Intersectional Pedagogy

Intersectional Pedagogy: Creative Education Practices for Gender and Peace Work teaches educators to use innovative learning methods to encourage students to rethink culture, gender, race, sexual orientation, and social class with a deep awareness of accessible language as a means of communication across disagreements.

With a focus on emancipatory critical pedagogy, as well as tools to promote sustainable peace and human rights advocacy, the book's main objective is to examine and present methods that can help students address rapidly changing social situations. Recent developments under discussion include the #MeToo and #WhyIDidntReport campaigns to counter sexual violence, campaigns to support refugees and migrants, and other human rights issues. The book examines how theory can be translated into practice and how various dilemmas pertaining to young people navigating a changing world can be successfully addressed in the classroom.

This book is an ideal reading for researchers and postgraduate students in education. It is written for practitioners in peace education and for those within traditional and alternative academia who wish to promote intersectional awareness in their teaching.

Gal Harmat is an educator, innovation adviser, and researcher in gender, emancipatory and peace education, and peace work. She was the 2018 Georg Arhold Visiting Research Professor at the Georg Eckert Institute for International Textbook Research in Braunschweig, Germany.

Routledge Research in Educational Equality and Diversity

Books in the series include:

Youth in Education
The necessity of valuing ethnocultural diversity
Christiane Timmerman, Noel Clycq, Marie McAndrew, Alhassane Balde, Luc Braekmans, Sara Mels

Black Men in Law School
Unmatched or Mismatched?
Darrell D. Jackson

British Pakistani Boys, Education and the Role of Religion
In the Land of the Trojan Horse
Karamat Iqbal

Gender in Learning and Teaching
Feminist Dialogues Across International Boundaries
Edited by Carol A. Taylor, Chantal Amade-Escot and Andrea Abbas

Nationality and Ethnicity in an Israeli School
A Case Study of Jewish-Arab Students
Dalya Yafa Markovich

Intersectional Pedagogy
Creative Education Practices for Gender and Peace Work
Gal Harmat

Schools as Queer Transformative Spaces
Global Narratives on Sexualities and Genders
Jón Ingvar Kjaran and Helen Sauntson

For more information about this series, please visit: www.routledge.com/Routledge-Research-in-Educational-Equality-and-Diversity/book-series/RREED

Intersectional Pedagogy
Creative Education Practices for Gender and Peace Work

Gal Harmat

First published 2020
by Routledge
2 Park Square, Milton Park, Abingdon, Oxon OX14 4RN

and by Routledge
52 Vanderbilt Avenue, New York, NY 10017

Routledge is an imprint of the Taylor & Francis Group, an informa business

First issued in paperback 2021

© 2020 Gal Harmat

The right of Gal Harmat to be identified as author of this work has been asserted by her in accordance with sections 77 and 78 of the Copyright, Designs and Patents Act 1988.

With the exception of Chapters 1 and 2, no part of this book may be reprinted or reproduced or utilised in any form or by any electronic, mechanical, or other means, now known or hereafter invented, including photocopying and recording, or in any information storage or retrieval system, without permission in writing from the publishers.

Chapters 1 and 2 of this book are available for free in PDF format as Open Access from the individual product page at www.routledge.com. It has been made available under a Creative Commons Attribution-Non Commercial-No Derivatives 4.0 license.

Trademark notice: Product or corporate names may be trademarks or registered trademarks, and are used only for identification and explanation without intent to infringe.

British Library Cataloguing in Publication Data
A catalogue record for this book is available from the British Library

Library of Congress Cataloging-in-Publication Data
A catalog record has been requested for this book

ISBN: 978-0-367-33380-5 (hbk)
ISBN: 978-1-03-208848-8 (pbk)
ISBN: 978-0-429-31951-8 (ebk)

Typeset in Bembo
by Taylor & Francis Books

To the memory of Henry H. Arnhold,
who made this world a better place with his
unwavering belief in creative critical education
and sustainable peace,
and to Judith Harmat, without whom this book
would never have been possible.

Contents

Acknowledgments ix

1 Introductions: Critical pedagogy and the intersectional complexities of names 1

  Naming the background 8
  Naming the conflict 11
  Gendered names 14
  Names and migration 17
  Conclusions 18

2 Practical gender in critical pedagogy: Analyzing everyday objects 23

  Gender in the academic (and development and peace work) field 24
  Gender analysis based on the relevance of everyday objects 27
  Handling resistance with feminist critical pedagogy practices 29
  Femininities and masculinities 34
  Power relations, objectification and reclaiming 37
  Relationships, love, and sisterhood 39
  Sexuality and rape culture 41
  Conclusions 45

3 Practical critical pedagogy: Developing educational materials on human rights and gender for children with students 50

  The human rights education course program 51
  The participants 54

The dilemma of language: all languages are not equal 55
Negotiating language issues of free speech 64
Conclusion 65

4   Creating images: Discovering hidden gender stereotypes
    about the self and the Other   68

   Gender-based stereotypes 69
   The mechanism of stereotyping 70
   The method 73
   National identity stereotypes override gender stereotypes 77
   Discussion of results 78
   Follow-up research on gender stereotypes 81
   Conclusion 84

Index   88

Acknowledgments

This book was written during a six-month visiting professorship at the Georg Eckert Institute for International Textbook Research (GEI) in Brunswick, Germany. The professorship was funded by the Georg Arnhold Program on Education for Sustainable Peace, instituted at the GEI by the late Henry Arnhold (1921–2018). I am also indebted to the support of Judith Harmat, who made the work on this book possible.

Many thanks to all whose work, editing and support helped me to write this book, especially Galia Zalmanson Levi, Wibke Westermeyer, Wendy Anne Kopisch, Katharina Baier, and Meyrick Payne.

To my love Morris Horesh and to my beloved Orka.

Gal Harmat
Tel Aviv, June 2019

1 Introductions

Critical pedagogy and the intersectional complexities of names

Writing the introduction to a book is not all that different from introducing a new group of students to one of my courses in gender and critical pedagogy, even if students are not my only target readership here. Those in a class before me may, or may not, already have an idea about what I teach, and they will probably have expectations of some kind, hopes, inhibitions, or perhaps even fears. Similarly, you, as the reader of this book, have purchased, borrowed, or downloaded this book with a certain expectation in mind, a pre-formed idea as to what this book is about. Perhaps you saw it advertised by the publisher, it may have been recommended to you, or perhaps you have simply judged the book by its cover. Either way, the ideas already present in your mind as you embark upon this introduction will be paramount to your perception and understanding of the content and may possibly shape the impact—or lack thereof—of this book on your own work and thinking.

This introduction will not simply introduce the topic of the book as a classical introduction. Instead, it will combine the first chapter of the book with introduction by focusing on how to start a workshop or a course. This is the way I often open my courses and learning workshops. We will begin, then, by examining the very concept of introductions in the widest sense, with a special focus on the function of names: the names that individuals are given at birth, usually by their parents or extended family, and that are often chosen because of their significance. People's names are imbued with meaning, with symbolism, with cultural—and often religious—meaning, which for some may carry positive connotations while others may find a certain name at best aseptic or, at worst, frightening. And in most cases, your name is the first aspect of your person that others experience.

By reflecting on the origins, meanings, and effects of our names, such prejudices can be nipped in the bud at the beginning of a course and thus serve not only the simple pragmatic purpose of introducing students to one another, rapidly building trust within the group by encouraging participants and facilitator to remember each other's names, but also highlight from the beginning the intersectional complexities inherent in the bearing, speaking, and perceiving of other people's names. Think about your own name. Have your parents or those who raised you told you why they chose this name for you? What possible ideas about the child and adult you would become were inherent in or presupposed by this name? Does it carry with it assumptions, expectations, associations, and, if so, how might these have impacted your life so far in your own specific sociopolitical context? Does your name carry with it implicit privileges or disadvantages? Who students are, where they come from, and what they do is relevant and often determines a great deal of the content of the course and the process of learning and creating knowledge together. This encompasses questions of who gave an individual their name, its meaning, provenance, and what historical, cultural, ethnic, religious, and gender contexts the name carries for them. In addition to asking what they like about and identify with their name, the method presented in this chapter serves as an introduction to critical education practices and explores how these practices are used in different contexts.

Our intersectional identities will determine the extent to which we will be challenged by this book and how it will resonate with us. This book will therefore not have the same effect on all readers. This introduction seeks to translate theories of critical pedagogy into educational practice, and to use this practice as a metaphor to show how this book can be implemented by education practitioners. It takes the critical practice of name analysis to explore with students their (and others) racial, ethnic, gender, sexual orientation, class, ability, marital status, and other identity characteristics and stereotypes that are crucial and relevant to their work and studies. The act of integrating who the students are, what they do, and are passionate about into the beginning of the course underscores that all experiences are equal and relevant in the class, in an atmosphere of sharing our experiences, backgrounds, and opinions (Clegg & Rowland, 2010; Kincheloe, McLaren, Steinberg, & Monzó, 2017).

Name-story sharing and name analysis is a method that aims to build bridges and encourage open and trusting dialogue. It is an educational practice in which participants and students of a course, workshop, or dialogue encounter share their name stories and are able to question, challenge, and explore identity, language, heritage, privileges, and (power) relations right from the beginning. It allows participants to reflect on the histories, traditions, and backgrounds that they are coming from, present whatever they would like to the group, and explore stereotypes they may have about others and themselves. In this book, I argue that encouraging participants to "bring" themselves and their diverse intersectional identity into the classroom creates an open atmosphere that allows for learning on a different level, the intellectual level (analysis of context and culture), which enables rich first-hand learning. This intellectual learning is woven together with emotional and social learning about identities, stereotypes, and prejudices in regard to names, backgrounds, and intersectional identity and individual and group reflection. The learning process itself is thus contextualized and linked to both the content and analytical and emotional framework of multicultural and diverse analysis.

In my educational work I am therefore particularly interested in phenomena such as names that act as "empty frames," to be "filled" in everyday life by what might be associated with them. This book presents structures and frameworks that can be used in a variety of subject areas and in relation to myriad topics relating to gender, social change, and peace studies. In this introductory chapter, I take the example of names and show how raising an awareness of their intersectional complexities can be an entry point to critical analysis. However, names are just one example of the framework that we carry around with us for others to "fill"; these can also be accents or dialects, styles of clothing, language usage, skin color, and so on; the list is inexhaustible as this method can be applied to almost any object, habitus, cultural ritual, context, or idea.

The fundamental term "intersectionality" was coined in 1989 by Kimberlé Crenshaw. In her academic teaching and her book *Mapping the Margins: Intersectionality, Identity Politics, and Violence against Women of Color*, she shows how systems of oppression operate differently depending on the specific cross-section of gender and race experienced by an individual or group of people. Crenshaw refers to this as "double oppression," as in the case, for example, of black women, who often experience discrimination both as a person of color and as a woman. Crenshaw's work opened up the field of gender studies and ethnography to the deep complexities of identity and discrimination (identity politics). Intersectional awareness in the field of education is valuable in that it helps educators and peace workers to design their courses and classes to fit the very specific intersectional needs and interests of their students. In peace work, in particular, this is particularly important because such contexts (refugee camps, peace negotiations, and development interventions) derive from and are traditionally built upon concepts of ethnicity, language, race, and culture. By introducing an intersectional approach to teaching and peace work, for example, the content matter being addressed in the classroom, peace workshops, or mediation processes can be brought into context with the specific and relevant complexities of individual and group identities. Intersectional awareness also helps to navigate contradictions by moving beyond binary thought patterns and male–female or black-and-white dichotomized categories of thinking.

Just as intersectional work in the classroom and in mediation processes takes a concept rooted in academia and applies it to the everyday and necessary practice of negotiating deeply complex and entrenched situations, so this book has originated in my work as a university professor and peace facilitator, and seeks to bridge the divide between theory and practice. It is therefore written first and foremost for practitioners in peace education but also for those working in more traditional academic spheres who wish to raise the level of intersectional awareness in their fields. Such academics are in a unique position to bring about social change via human rights education and intersectional approaches. They may be particularly effective when not restricting the transmission of knowledge to the privileged students sitting in their lecture halls and seminar rooms, but when making use of widely accessible communication technology and social media, such as Twitter, Instagram, Facebook, and YouTube. While there is controversial debate about the peacebuilding potential and risks inherent in social media, there is no doubt that its high level of accessibility and interactive possibilities widens opportunities for marginalized people and groups.

Knowledge about anything in the world, from how to repair a car, braid hair, build a house, or speak eight languages, is—from the point of view of critical pedagogy—relevant to the course material and can serve as effective examples via which to explore key issues. Ultimately, the practices presented in this book seek to unveil how everything we do and say—or do not do or say—is based upon the specific ideological framework unique to every individual and informed by that person's own particular knowledge, experience, fears, and values. These practices aim to render visible such unspoken or subconscious ideologies that inform our everyday communication and actions. Students who thus become more intersectionally aware have a far greater potential for success in intervention and mediation processes as well as in educational contexts, thanks to their deeper insight into the complexities of human identity and processes of—often inadvertent—discrimination. Clegg & Rowland claim that the link between the different types of learning can be exchanged with the term "kindness." They suggest that teaching and practicing kindness in academic institutions is a political, radical act, and argue that linking the emotional to the intellectual is subversive of neoliberal values. They reject the binary segregation between academic or intellectual work and emotion or reason, and the associated gendered racial and cultural binaries of learning (Clegg & Rowland, 2010).

The student's experiences thus serve as part of the curriculum, and the learning materials are thus part of their own experiences. The analysis and reflection, and later the translation into educational practices, is conducted in the language format that is most convenient to the students. Similarly, this book will explore complex concepts and use language that is accessible to wide audiences as a pedagogical act that is critical and radical (Kincheloe, 2012). One of the key arguments of this book is, therefore, that if we are truly engaging in intersectional work, we need to communicate in accessible language rather than in what has been referred to as "hegemonic language." To what extent is it possible, however, to publish with renowned academic publishers if one does not conform to traditional conventions of academic writing? The book aspires to challenge peace- and gender-related mediation processes and structures established in the academic world, especially in conflict areas or regions with significant economic disparities.

Critical pedagogy encourages a conscious educational synthesis with the individual and group experience in regard to place, action, or involvement. A critical pedagogy analysis emphasizes intersectional aspects of social experience, drawing from its lessons learned and actions (Crenshaw, 1991; hooks, 1991, 1994; Gerhards & Hans, 2009). Furthermore, critical pedagogy scholars argue that reflections on critical practices and the learner's experiences in relation to power dynamics and an exploration of backgrounds provide a way to define and recognize teaching and learning styles that are gendered and culturally relevant (Apple, 1993, 1983; Ladson-Billings, 1995, 2014). When students/participants are encouraged to share their historical narratives, backgrounds, and the way they perceive their identities it legitimizes who they are in regard to the learning material. The curriculum or learning materials based on their presented experiences encourage a fluid understanding of culture, and a teaching practice that explicitly engages questions of equity, politics, and justice which become relevant and therefore engaging, enriching, and inspiring, ultimately waging change (Apple, 1993; Ladson-Billings, 1995, 2014).

The reflective, self-ethnographic, and participatory critical observation of group dynamics and one's own work is part of a long tradition of feminist and participatory action research and represents the ideology, theory, and practice of critical and feminist pedagogy (Kincheloe, 2012).

Students' involvement, self-research, and relations between concept and object and between signifier and signified are challenged by such a research method. The assumptions are that social power relations are not objective and cannot be factual but are always indicative of hegemonic power structures. The language and jargon of academic disciplines are tools to maintain the status quo (Gor Ziv, 2013). In the following chapters, therefore, I use accessible language and seek to make my reflections and analyses of the practices relatable to the reader's experience. The aim is to encourage readers to use these practices, draw their own conclusions, and to enable educators to translate their own preferred theories into educational practices (Kincheloe, McLaren, Steinberg, & Monzó, 2017).

At the beginning of a workshop with refugees and education students, in which a book on human rights was to be developed, one of the participants began: "My name is Abdulla. I love my name as it is the second strongest (most powerful) and most beautiful name a person in Islam can have. It represents strength and my culture." During the group discussion one of the German students commented that she was surprised by Abdulla's story as many people in her community are afraid of this name, and similar names, associating them with negative stereotypes: "It is a terrorist name for me." It is this necessary space for discussion and dialogue surrounding the inherent and latent stereotypes people bring with them that forms the foundation of the practices explored in the following.

Alford states that ethnographic research has not yet identified a single society that abstains from using naming practices, and that names signify realities, cultures, and values (Alford, 1988). Since everybody possesses a name and it is a universal commonality, name-sharing is an example of how language plays a major role in international educational settings, such as courses, academic workshops, and dialogue encounters. The meaning of the participants' names and how they are analyzed and perceived sometimes affects the ways in which they act and behave, and whether they can thrive in the class or course and indicate the complex, multi-layered identities, hidden conflicts, ethnic and cultural tensions, and prejudices they bring with them to class (Crenshaw, 1991; Gor Ziv, 2013).

Names are crucial to the process of introduction and getting to know one another. Names help us to create order and structure our conception of the world. It is through naming that we make the world comprehensible (Lévi-Strauss, 1996). My academic courses, workshops, and training, like most others, usually begin with participants and students introducing themselves and their names. This introduction helps the participants to remember each other's names. Due to language differences within a class, this is often very revealing, especially with regard to meaning and etymology. Interestingly, on some occasions, this process humanizes the other by demonstrating that participants would choose to avoid sharing their name's meaning, or just lessen its significance.

Many names, especially in the Global South but also in traditional societies in the Global North, have deep connotations to historical, ethnic, political, and religious positions. In many cases names serve as metaphors for national and religious concepts (Barry & Harper, 1995). A metaphor is the use of one thing as representative or symbolic of another. It is a figure of speech that conveys an analogy between ideas. A metaphor carries meaning via association, via resemblance or via comparison to the denoted object. Lakoff and Johnson (1980) talk about "dead metaphors" to describe metaphors that are normally unnoticed since they are so regularly used. Dead metaphors are no longer seen as metaphors but are treated as a linguistic expression, as a word. Such metaphors become conventions that do not require an interpretation or comparison between two fields of meanings. Exploring the metaphorical aspects of names enables participants to look into our deep culture and how it is represented in our everyday use of language (Galtung & MacQueen, 2008). Names are usually such dead metaphors; we know that they have meaning but we do not think about them in our daily lives. However, in the process of the course or workshop, the participants can search for their deep meanings and thereby reanimate the dead metaphor. Dafne's example from an online course on gender and peacebuilding is illustrative here:

> My name is Dafne, with an "f" instead of a "ph" and it's "Dafne like the one from Scooby Doo." The last phrase is exactly how I introduce myself many times in order for people from my own country and even my relatives to know how to write or pronounce it (I have an uncle that cannot pronounce my name and calls me Flounder, like the one from The Little Mermaid or Waffle, I am not kidding!). Dafne or Daphne is a female name and means "laurel." It derives from a minor figure in Greek mythology known as a naiad—a type of female nymph associated with fountains, wells, springs, streams, brooks and other freshwater bodies. The mythological narrative states that because of her beauty, Daphne attracted the attention and ardor of the god Apollo. As she did not want to be with him, she asked her father to transform her into a laurel tree. My father (deceased) chose my name and, unfortunately, I never asked him why he did; what I do know is that my mother had

another name in mind, but she agreed because she liked it. One of my uncles asked my mother to not use the ph, because "we are not English speakers," as he said. What I like about my name is that it is unique in my hometown and even in Mexico. What I don't like is the fact that many people cannot spell it: Dacne, Dagne, Dafani.

Dafne's name story opened up the meaning and interpretation of her name that served right from the beginning as an intersectional identity analysis. Through such analyses, one can learn about family relations, ethnicity, power, and language background, in addition to cultural foundations and gender. Dafne was also willing to share that her father passed away and her sensitivity to changes in her name by other people seem disrespectful to his memory for her. This practice not only allows for its introduction at the beginning of the workshop, but also enables the other students to get to know her better and to start exploring intersectionality analysis as a practice in the course.

"My name is Snow," shared a female student from the USA. "My parents wanted me to have a unique rare name that represents the location from which I am from that no one else shares." Children's names often strongly reflect the cultural, ideological, religious, and political values of their background, and symbolize the way parents would like to socialize their children with their own values (Alford, 1988), representing political, environmental, gender, social, and religious ideology. Oliver, Wood, & Bass suggest that liberals favor unique names that represent their cultural wealth and status while at the same time foregrounding their level of education. Conversely, conservatives choose traditional names that will distinguish their children as economically successful and represent money and power (Oliver, Wood, & Bass, 2015).

Naming the background

Lakoff and Johnson write about "meta-metaphors" that are used to structure our reality and create analogies between the concrete and the abstract. They form not just our language but also our conceptual maps and our understanding of reality (Lakoff & Johnson, 1980). In areas of ethnic and religious conflict such as Israel and Palestine, Bosnia-Herzegovina, the Democratic Republic of Congo, and Northern Iraq, names reflect people's background irrespective of whether it is openly discussed or obscured. A similar phenomenon of hidden knowledge regarding ethnic and religious background exists in the Republic of Ireland and Northern Ireland. A person's background and therefore religious affiliation is easily discernible based on accent, the spelling of their name, or the school she/he attended, even before this information is shared in a dialogue encounter.

Name introductions can empower marginalized sub-groups or individuals in the course group to share something unique about themselves or their culture, and to have voice and space right at the beginning of a course. Name-story sharing may also be used to legitimize religious or political views and positions. The critical educational practice of a circle in which all participants share whatever they choose to about their names enables the group to raise questions, concerns, and even prejudices right from the beginning of the process.

Guevara was a participant from Syria in a human rights children's book production workshop in Germany. He explained that his parents adore the revolutionary hero Che Guevara and named their oldest son after him to symbolize their admiration and hope that one day he would bring freedom to his country. Even people who do not think of Che Guevara as a positive figure could empathize with his parents' aspirations. By sharing his name story Guevara simultaneously highlights ideology and the legitimation of revolutionary sentiments.

In Israeli and Arab-Palestinian contexts, ethnicity, religion and relative piety, the political views of parents, social and economic background, class, and gender are all exposed merely by the utterance of one's name. Identity is immediately unveiled via a commonplace introduction. For example, the Hebrew masculine names Erez (cedar) and Gilad (mountain) are commonly read as deriving from Zionist backgrounds; at once close to nature and predominantly secular. Beginning in the 1970s and continuing until the early 1990s it was fashionable to name Jewish-Israeli children after natural phenomena found within the country's borders, such as mountains and flora. This was done intentionally in order to "root" the children within Israeli culture and historical territory and to encourage their emotional and physical connection to the homeland. Such names were instrumentalized to represent the attachment of the Jewish people to their rightful, historical, homeland. They were also a continuation of a custom from the 1950s and 1960s of Jewish parents naming their children after historical figures and geographical locations mentioned in the Bible. Such names signified the return of the Jews to an historical land that was ordained to them by a biblical God. These names represent the power of the Jewish people and the continuation of the Jewish heritage in Israel through Hebrew masculine names like David, Shaul, and Shmuel. From the 1920s into the 1960s, the naming of children was part of the wider phenomenon of the creation and development of a series of symbols that represented the historical right of

Jews to the land of Israel, including the renewal of biblical names, the revival of Hebrew—the Jewish biblical language—and the reuse of biblical place names. Old Arabic names also carry volatile political significance, such as in the case of Haifa, Acco, and Gaza—the female name that signifies the Palestinian city which since 1948 has been situated in Israel.

Names can also share the background of a political situation and even serve as a symbol of colonialism or heritage. "My name is Atiano which means 'born at night,' but you can call me Grace as it is easier for you," said a South African student in a gender and peacebuilding training course for development workers in an international training course center in Austria. I asked her which name she preferred. She said that she likes her African name, but since it is hard for "Western people" to pronounce it she uses her Christian name. She shared that, during her childhood in apartheid-era South Africa, black people were not allowed to register their children without an official English name. She does not like the name Grace but uses it by default for people who have difficulties with her African name. Similarly, international or globally popular names are common in postwar countries or in conflict areas where parents would like to hide their child's mixed or marginalized ethnicity, as in the case of Jennifer from South Sudan, who participated in a workshop on peace education at the Austrian peace center, IPT:

> My name is Jennifer. It is a very easy name to say and no one can tell my ethnicity or background; no one can even tell if I am black or white. In my country there is ethnic cleansing against my ethnic group and since I am in favor of mixed marriages, I could be in danger of being killed by different groups. My parents named me Jennifer and changed my surname to an international name as well, so no one will know anything about me.

But even away from the threat of ethnicity-based persecution, globally viable names are given with a view to promoting world citizenship. "My name is Hannah," shared a German student at the University for Peace in Costa Rica:

> My parents named me Hannah, a Biblical Jewish, but also Christian and Muslim name, that is easy to pronounce and exists all around the world. This shows that they wanted me to be a citizen of the world, that people everywhere could say my name. I love it that when I am in Arab countries or even in Asia people find it easy to say my name and feel connected to it.

Naming the conflict

The sharing of name stories in a group can also serve to emphasize the shared humanity of participants coming from conflicting sides in mediation processes and dialogue encounters. Personal histories can thus be shared, recounted, and compared to the histories and names of the "others" (Johnson & Johnson, 1991). By telling personal and family histories, hostile and antagonistic feelings that arise when people from conflict zones express their political views can be addressed and perhaps overcome (Bar-On, 2006). Although the conversation surrounding name stories may conceal many aspects of the conflict and raise negative emotions like anger, fear, fury, and even in extreme cases hatred, still they allow people to listen to each other's personal narratives without having to argue on whether their story is "correct" or not, as is often the case when historical stories or political events and situations are examined (Bar-On & Adwan, 2004). Further, the name analysis exercise also helps the participants to remember each other's names and overcome the first step in a long process toward humanizing the "other." This has an enormous effect on the dialogue process, as Isra, a female Palestinian facilitator using these practices in dialogue encounters in Israel states:

> The one part of the dialogue encounter that makes me feel that I really hate this work and the Jewish people is the phase when the Jewish participants can't pronounce the Palestinian participants' names. Ugh, it says so much about language and power in this country that they can't even say their peers' names properly.

Here we see how name-story introductions can be one of the hardest steps in creating dialogue, particularly perhaps in a multicultural course where the access to the privileges of language and power are unequally distributed among the participants. It is often the case that participants from hegemonic groups who are unaware of the hegemony of their own language feel that they cannot, physically or emotionally, pronounce the "other" group's names correctly. For instance, a male student from a privileged background and a hegemonic European culture who was participating in a human rights children's book workshop that was conducted in his home town (in Western Europe) stated that he "just can't remember foreign names." He suggested either giving the refugee participants in the groups "easier names" or simply "remembering their faces." Another male student from the USA participating in a human rights course at the UN University for Peace in Costa Rica reacted angrily when I asked him to remember some of the fellow students' names: "It is impossible for me; I never encountered these names before," he protested, making it clear within the group that we were asking too much of him. This act of refusing to learn and memorize the names of people from diverse ethnic and racial groups sends a strong message to the non-hegemonic group. For those coming from the most marginalized language groups, the statement that one has "never heard that name before" renders members of such groups unimportant and invisible. Participants' names from strong groups are often remembered more easily by their peers, and by facilitators and professors.

The request to try and remember names from diverse cultures can result in fraught situations, especially in progressive universities that aim to diversify their student body but prefer students to adjust their names to the hegemonic language, and organizations where the failure to remember names that fall outside of the hegemonic power discourse can become particularly conflictual. This failure to remember the name of the "other," particularly in conflict areas, while in many cases perhaps no more than a result of poor memory skills or pure laziness, can also be symbolic of the power dynamic, indifference, ethnocentric values, or even colonialist practice.

Various political notions can also be conveyed via names with "militant" meanings such as "fight," "struggle," "power," or "victory." For example, the Hebrew name Oz, meaning "strength, powerful, courageous," refers culturally to military strength (a few elite military units are named Oz as well). The Arabic masculine name Jihad, meaning "holy war," represents a religious (and, from a Jewish perspective, militant) background. The female Arab name Fida, meaning "act of courage and bravery," similarly refers to the Jihad, or holy war. A 22-year-old Jewish-Israeli participant described her encounter with this name in a group of Israelis and Palestinians in Israel thus:

> I was shocked to find out that someone's name is Jihad. I always thought Jihad is a name of a terrorist who will blow himself up in our shopping mall. I thought to myself, what kind of crazy human-hating parents would name their son like that? I didn't talk to him, yet in the group he said very nice things, so I took a deep breath and asked him about the name … He explained that his parents were religious and that the name only bore meaning on the religious level and that it is a symbol of purity as well. I calmed down a little but not entirely. His name made me realize how distanced we are from each other and how little we know about the "other."

Introductions   13

Names also reveal a connection to shared geographical areas and cultural symbols, places where a war has taken place, or as a symbolic act that commemorates war, heroes, and conflict. In conflict zones, names and the act of naming can thus become "weaponized." "My name is Victor, after the victory of my ethnic group against the government," shares a male student from a West African country, in an international training course for development work in Austria. "My name symbolizes our victory and their loss and defeat. It is a strong name that can give power to those who fight."

According to Galtung, our deep culture is the internalized social constructions that are reflected in many of our habits and acts and are signified in our choices about what we do and how we do it. Names often represent deep cultures and are used as meta-metaphors. Such names demonstrate ways of thinking, feeling and acting in both societies on a very deep and rooted level (Galtung, 2017, Galtung & MacQueen, 2008). In this sense, names can also serve as monuments or as symbols of memory cultures. Several students in my courses from conflict zones have been given the name of someone who was killed in a war, an attack, or in a heroic act, demonstrating how names manifest a connection to meaningful political and cultural role models. Students share that they carry the obligations and sometimes burdens, but also the honor, of the person they are named after. Such stories can represent challenges to groups that are dealing with peacebuilding and mediation, but they also pave the way for participants' historical narratives and allow other members of the group to ask about specific individual ideologies and opinions. "I am named after my father's best friend, Bashar, who protected him and was killed during the war," said a Syrian student at the Austrian International Civilian Peacekeeping and Peacebuilding Training Programme (IPT). Many students were taken by surprise and asked the speaker about the responsibility and emotional burden. Bashar explained that it is a common practice and that he had never reflected on it. "It is there to remind me who I am and where I come from."

Some names are bilingual synonyms, sharing the same meaning but giving rise to conflicting narratives. The Arabic female name Watane means "homeland," referring to the Palestinian land. Palestinian parents give this name to daughters in order to emphasize the connection to their homeland Palestine and to "root" them within Palestinian culture. Names like Watane that carry national meanings became common among Palestinians in Israel as much as among the diaspora after the 1948 war and even more so after 1967. Likewise, the Hebrew female name Moledet has the same meaning, and is given to female children as a symbol of holding on steadfastly to the land. Palestinians and Jews thus refer to the same geographical piece of land; however, it is seen as this or that nation's exclusive homeland. Two further examples are the female Arabic name Amal and the female Hebrew name Tikva, both meaning "hope"; and the Arabic name Haiat and the Hebrew name Haim meaning "life." It is easier for Israelis and members of other hegemonic groups to remember names that are linguistically closer to theirs. The political choice of giving children names that are easier to pronounce by the hegemonic group determines one's potential identity, connection, and relationships (Lévi-Strauss, 1996). Some Jewish examples include Nir, meaning "green field"; Omer, originally a unit of dry measure referring to a sheaf, or an amount of grain large enough to require bundling; Yarden, Gilad, Gilboa, and Arbel are names of Israeli mountains underscoring the continuity between the Jewish people and the land, and the occupation of Israel both in biblical times and today. Similarly, names which carry political memory in the wake of wars, occupations, or peace accords were fashionable in Israel around major historical events, such as the female Jewish name Shlomit, meaning "peace."

We thus see that telling name stories and expanding on the meanings and uses of one's name are essential components of the dialogue process. They symbolize and reinforce the reality of conflict and power dynamics that are latent in language and knowledge and expose the fact that many participants are excluded by the structural imbalances of a dominant discourse that cannot even pronounce their name, and therefore neglects to address them.

Gendered names

Names also represent power, control, and future success based on gender. According to Oliver, Wood, & Bass, liberals in the United States prefer birth names with "softer, feminine" sounds while conservatives favor names with "harder, masculine" phonemes. These findings have significant implications for both studies of consumption and debates about ideology and political fragmentation in the United States (Oliver, Wood, & Bass, 2015).

Those with "soft" feminine names are less likely to be hired for what are considered powerful and dominant jobs such as political positions, management, or high-trust appointments (Barry & Harper, 1995; Whissell, 2001).

> My name is Rafael. As I have travelled quite a lot, as well as living abroad, I can say that I consider my first name international. It is

easy to pronounce, and people do not really know where I come from. What is clear about my name is its gender, as the female version would be Rafaelle or Rafaela.

Similar masculine names from around the world (Daniel, Gabriel, Luis) are rendered in their feminine form by appending the name with a vowel, typically "a" or "e." The "original" name is masculine by default and the ending feminizes it. Simone de Beauvoir (1989 [1952]) argued that "humanity is male, and man defines woman not in herself but as relative to him." Rafaela, Gabriela, and Daniela are examples of names derived from masculine versions rather than conversely. They are but a handful of examples among millions of others that testify to the patriarchy that has been passed across generations and is symbolized in names. Names can thus represent and symbolize the gendered views of parents whose naming of their child can be seen as a microcosmic reflection of society. In addition to being given the names of sturdy trees and lofty mountains, males are also named after powerful animals, such as Channing, Lowell, Phelan, and Rudolph/Ralph variations, all of which derive from "wolf." Similarly, the primordial meaning of the name Draco is the Greek "dragon" or the protector of or from one. Several names, such as Philip and the feminized Philippa, derive from the root "horse protection," while Rosamund is a name whose meaning has shifted from that of protection to equine beauty and elegance.

Women are typically named after smaller, more delicate, and symbolically non-threatening animals, such as doves, which symbolize peace and purity, for example Paloma, Jona, Frauna, or Jamima/Jemima. Yara is a common name in Spain and South America with Arabic origins, meaning "butterfly." The female names Vanessa, Kimana, and Farasha also derive from words for butterfly. Female and male names represent and reinforce traditional values and societal expectations. If we consider the energy and intention behind names and compare a lion or bear to a butterfly, we can link the future expectations and the social roles that are premeditated for men as protectors, defenders, and strong public figures and women as protected, delicate creatures who need to be guarded.

One particularly vivid example is the convention of female names that symbolize honor, purity, and virginity in the family, community, and the nation, such as the name Catherine, of French origin meaning pure or clear. According to the name-meaning app *mamajunction* there are 519 female names that signify purity, from Tahira, which means pure and clean, to Svetlana, meaning "pure and light." A shortlist of names from across the world that symbolize female purity and innocence are Alma, Chepa, Caylen, Dalaja, Anisa, Aneesha, and Tristyn, meaning a virtuous and pure virgin. Names for women also derive from floral terms, beautiful natural phenomena, and objects that are pleasing to the eye. "My name is Meshi, meaning 'silk.' It represents the softness and gentleness that the female child is supposed to have or acquire, and I feel that all my life my community expected me to be as delicate and beautiful as silk," said a student in a gender course at the Academic College of Society and the Arts in Netanya, Israel.

The Arabic female names Hitam and Nihaya, meaning "end" and "final," are usually given to girls born after "too many" girls had already been born to their parents. These names are said to be given in order to stop the stream of girls' births on an energetic level. They represent the strong social preference for boys (especially as a first-born) and the fact that a man who fathers "too many" girls is ridiculed in many parts of the world (Nwokocha, 2007).

A study conducted in the 1980s in the United States and followed up on in the early 1990s measured frequencies of unisex names in Pennsylvania in 1960 and 1990. Barry and Harper (2014) concluded that unisex or non-sex or non-gender revealing naming is increasingly popular. The frequency of unisex names was four times higher in 1990 than in the previous time period surveyed. Barry and Harper contend that people strongly preferred to give unisex names to girls and were reluctant to name boys with unisex names, visible and pronounced masculinity being considered a positive attribute. In a world where men own the majority of businesses and fill most of the highest governmental and corporate positions (Acker 2004), having a masculine or gender-neutral name can be a strategic advantage for both males and females. Some of my students have reported on this: "[my name is] Daneyra. My father loves the word 'donaire' (grace, charm) which can be a masculine name. My parents knew I was a baby girl, so they decided to make that word feminine. They played around with the letters and Daneyra came out." Names like Daneyra, Yarden (after the Jordan river), and Gal (a wave in the sea) create confusion and are meant to blur the child's gender, particularly in the case of females. Female participants often state that their parents would have preferred a boy but since they were born, their parents gave them a masculine name. Others state that their parents wanted to protect them from being a girl, so they named them with a unisex name to enable her to pass as male. According to Duffy and Ridinger (1981), gender-masking, the allocation of unisex names to female children, protects women from sexism in the workplace, school, and social life, and may determine their social role and position.

Names and migration

Second-generation migrants' first names reveal the acculturation and assimilation processes of first-generation migrants, as well as how migrants define themselves based on their cultures and languages, both of their host and of their origins. First names are often chosen freely by immigrants and encompass identity, ethnic, and religious characteristics not associated with any material cost (Lieberson, 2000). In their article "From Hasan to Herbert: Name-Giving Patterns of Immigrant Parents between Acculturation and Ethnic Maintenance," Jurgen Gerhards and Silke Hans claim that (first) names can be a symbol and an indicator that migrants feel a sense of belonging to a particular ethnic group. They examined first-name giving in three different immigrant groups in Germany. They found out that patterns of acculturation and self-definitions of identity can be observed in the patterns of first-name giving. People who migrated from Southern and Western Europe gave their children German names more often than people who migrated from Turkey (Gerhards & Hans, 2009). Bertrand and Mullainathan (2004) demonstrate that people with names perceived by some as typically black in the US are discriminated against much more frequently, and that black people with non-black names or white names face less discrimination in the workplace and are invited to more job interviews.

Talking with migrants and refugees about their names thus opens up a sensitive dialogue about discrimination, racism, and their family's values and views. As names are often culturally exclusive, local or international migrants make a political choice whether to project assimilation, acculturation, and integration, or to give their child a name maintaining their origin culture, language, and ethnicity. "My name is Anas. My parents wanted me to have an Arabic name although I was born in France," shares a male student (27) at the International Development Workshop in Austria. "In Hebrew my name means rapist. They wanted me to be named this in order to avoid my ever hooking up with a Jewish woman ... They also wanted me to have a strong or significant name in a foreign country, so I will not forget where I'm from or who I am."

"That's funny," a female student (24) at the same course reacts:

> I'm also an immigrant in France and I have a very French name, Sophie, to symbolize integration and that my parents gave up their past and left their heritage and language in Vietnam. We speak French at home and they gave me a French name so I'll have an easier time integrating. They even changed part of their last name

to something more French so people will not discriminate. It works well, and people assume that I'm French and invite me to job interviews.

Asian immigrants in the US often give their children names perceived to be "white American" in order to have them pronounced correctly, since they feel that their language is not valued as much as the hegemonic culture. By giving their children American names they feel more assimilated and see themselves as American first and foremost. People from Latin America, on the other hand, tend to maintain their ethnic and cultural names and to define themselves as Latinos due to the proximity to Latin America and the visible and known culture and language of Latinos in the US. Many also perceive themselves as a large minority. Thus, rather than being seen as a risk, it is rather considered an opportunity and privilege for a child to be known as Latino in their community (Lieberson, 2000). Similarly, a female student (25) at a human rights and gender course at Haceteppe University, Turkey, shared:

> My name was Hannah. My parents who emigrated from Iraq gave me this name, so I would pass well in our new European country, but I changed my name to Hamida to symbolize that I am a Muslim. I want to carry my identity with my name, and I would like everybody else to know that I'm a Muslim and Arab.

These three examples highlight the discourse and constant dialogue around names within migration processes. Interestingly, it seems that when non-immigrants name their child with a foreign or unique name, they are considered to project creativity and imagination, while immigrants who give their child a more unusual name are perceived to be insufficiently integrated.

Conclusions

In the educational practice of debriefing names, some students analyze their own names critically, while others present their name implicitly accepting their own cultural milieu and status quo. During the analysis, the students are asked to refrain from analyzing other names and to only give meanings and explanations when asked. Allowing them to reflect about the deep culture of their names and the way their own name represents more or less power can be an inspiring but also a painful process. Each student takes part as much as they would like and exposes as much as they are comfortable with. For some it is easy, while for others it is difficult, arguing that analyzing their name can be disrespectful to their parents, culture, and community. Participants therefore first analyze their names and then allow time for conversation and thoughts about the process. This sets the stage for a dialogue about social constructions, intersectionality, race theory, and critical analysis of peacebuilding and development interventions. The namestory exercise allows participants to explore their hidden stereotypes, present their histories and heritage, and recount something about their parents and their political, religious, and ideological views. Exploring names together facilitates a dialogue process right from the beginning of the encounter or workshop about hidden and invisible assumptions about the "other."

I have begun this book with an introduction that looks into the intricacies of introductions themselves—in this case, the functions of names—in order to reveal right from the outset how important it is to maintain a critical awareness of how quickly we form impressions and prejudices on the basis of the use of words and language, among other things. There is no one way in which this book might prove useful, but I hope that it might be used in the following three ways.

The first is the use of the practices described in this book for practitioners, university professors, teachers, informal educators, and peace workers. I hope that the structures and frameworks for teaching designs presented here might provide a space for subject-specific content required by curricula or peace intervention work. What I present in Chapter 2 as a gender-object analysis, for example, might be implemented elsewhere as a conflict-related or ageism-related analysis, or an examination of how different sexual orientations are depicted in a children's book, for example. Similarly, the analysis of stereotypes through the practice of ice-cream sculpturing and fast drawing discussed in Chapter 4 can be shifted into a discourse about stereotypes but also other societal issues, such as ableism, adultism, and classism. My hope is that the readers of this book will use these practices and methods for their own purposes and in accordance with their own needs.

The second way in which I hope this book might prove useful is in the inspiration of storytelling. The process of storytelling by students, teachers, peace workers, and refugees can be extremely valuable. Everyone has a story; a narrative that others can learn from or be inspired by. The objective here is to create knowledge based on experiences, and to encourage others to develop new knowledge together with learners based on their experiences.

Finally, this book seeks to illustrate some ways in which theory can be translated into practice, with the aim of revealing to students and workshop participants how formal ideologies and theories can be made relevant to their everyday lives, by conducting a gender-related analysis of an everyday object, for example. Innovative experiential learning encourages students to actively think and analyze rather than passively absorb information via rote-learning.

But the practices and methods presented here will not in themselves provide the answers or solutions to the societal problems of our time. They seek to raise questions and to foster conversations that shape a critical intersectional lens through which we look at the world. This book will probably not directly change reality by itself, but I hope it will unveil means by which we can change the way we talk and think about our reality. Ultimately, it is such shifts in thought and discourse that bring about changes to reality itself, toward gender equity, human rights for all people, and sustainable peace based on social justice.

References

Acker, J. 2004. "Hierarchies, Jobs, Bodies: A Theory of Gendered Organizations." In *The Gendered Society Reader*, ed. by M. S. Kimmel with A. Aronson. New York: Oxford University Press.
Alford, R.D. 1988. *Naming and Identity: A Cross-cultural Study of Personal Naming Practices*. New Haven, CT: HRAF Press.
Apple, M. 1993. *Official Knowledge*. New York: Routledge.
Apple, M. & Weiss, L. 1983. *Ideology and Practice in Schooling*. Philadelphia: Temple University Press.
Bar-On, D. 2006. *Tell Your Life: Creating Dialog Between Jews and Germans*. Budapest: Central European University Press.
Bar-On, D. & Adwan, S. 2004. *Shared History Project: A PRIME Example of Peace-Building*.
Barry, H.B. & Harper, A.S. 1994. "Sex Differences in Linguistic Origins of Personal Names." In *Names New and Old*, ed. by E. Wallace McMullen, 281–300. Madison, NJ: Penny Press.
Barry, H.B. & Harper, A.S. 1995. "Increased Choice of Female Phonetic Attributes in First Names." *Sex Roles* 32: 809–819. doi.org/10.1007/BF01560190
Barry, H.B. & Harper, A.S. 2000. "Three Last Letters Identify Most Female First Names." *Psychological Reports* 87(1): 48–54. https://doi.org/10.2466/pr0.2000.87.1.48
Barry, H.B. & Harper, A.S. 2014. "Unisex Names for Babies Born in Pennsylvania 1990–2010." *Names* 62(1): 13–22.
Bertrand, M. & Mullainathan, S. 2004. "Are Emily and Greg More Employable than Lakisha and Jamal? A Field Experiment on Labor Market Discrimination." *American Economic Review* 94(4): 991–1013.

Crenshaw, K. 1989. "Demarginalizing the Intersection of Race and Sex: A Black Feminist Critique of Antidiscrimination Doctrine, Feminist Theory and Antiracist Politics." *University of Chicago Legal Forum*: 1989, Article 8.
Crenshaw, K. 1991. "Mapping the Margins: Intersectionality, Identity Politics, and Violence against Women of Color." *Stanford Law Review* 43(6): 1241–1299.
Clegg, S. & Rowland, S. 2010. "Kindness in Pedagogical Practice and Academic Life." *British Journal of Sociology of Education* 31(6): 719–735. Retrieved from http://www.jstor.org/stable/25758494
de Beauvoir, Simone. 1989 [1952]. *The Second Sex*. New York: Vintage Books.
Duffy, J.C., & Ridinger, B. 1981. "Stereotyped Connotations of Masculine and Feminine Names." *Sex Roles* 7: 25–33.
Galtung, J. 2017. *Deep Culture, Deep Structure, Deep Nature, Three Pillars of Peace Theory and Peace Practice*. Grenzach-Wyhlen: Transcend University Press.
GaltungJ. & MacQueen, G. 2008: *Globalizing God: Religion, Spirituality and Peace*. Grenzach-Wyhlen: Transcend University Press.
Gerhards, J. & Hans, S. 2009. "From Hasan to Herbert: Name-Giving Patterns of Immigrant Parents between Acculturation and Ethnic Maintenance." *American Journal of Sociology* 114(4): 1102–1128. doi:10.1086/595944
Gor Ziv, H. 2013. *Feminist Critical Pedagogy and Education for a Culture of Peace*. Mofet.
hooks, b. 1991. *Yearning: Race, Gender, and Cultural Politics*. London: Turnaround.
hooks, b. 1994. *Teaching to Transgress: Education as the Practice of Freedom*. New York: Routledge.
Kincheloe, J. 2012. "Critical Pedagogy in the Twenty-First Century: Evolution for Survival." *Counterpoints* 422: 147–183. Retrieved from http://www.jstor.org/stable/42981758
Kincheloe, J.L., McLaren, P., Steinberg, S.R., & Monzó, L. 2017. "Critical Pedagogy and Qualitative Research: Advancing the Bricolage." In N.K. Denzin & Y.S. Lincoln (eds), *The SAGE Handbook of Qualitative Research* (5th ed.), 235–260. Thousand Oaks, CA: SAGE.
Ladson-Billings, G. 1995. "Toward a Theory of Culturally Relevant Pedagogy." *American Educational Research Journal*, 32(3): 465–491. https://doi.org/10.3102/00028312032003465
Ladson-Billings, G. 2014. "Culturally Relevant Pedagogy 2.0: a.k.a. The Remix." *Harvard Educational Review* 84(1): 74–84.
Lakoff, G. &Johnson, M. 1980. *Metaphors We Live By*. Chicago: University of Chicago.
Lévi-Strauss, C. 1996 [1962]. *The Savage Mind*. Oxford: Oxford University Press.
Lieberson, S. 2000. *A Matter of Taste: How Names, Fashions and Culture Change*. New Haven, CT: Yale University Press.
Nwokocha, E. 2007. "Male-Child Syndrome and the Agony of Motherhood among the Igbo of Nigeria." *International Journal of Sociology of the Family* 33 (1): 219–234. Retrieved from http://www.jstor.org/stable/23070771

Oliver, E., T. Wood, & Bass, A. 2015. "Liberellas versus Konservatives: Social Status, Ideology, and Birth Names in the United States." *Political Behavior* 38. 10.1007/s11109-11015-9306-9308.

Whissell, Cynthia. 2001. "Cues to Referent Gender in Randomly Constructed Names." *Perceptual and Motor Skills* 93: 856–858.

2 Practical gender in critical pedagogy
Analyzing everyday objects

This chapter offers a theoretical and methodological framework for implementing feminist critical pedagogy in compulsory courses in gender studies. The method examined presents a gender analysis of daily objects by students as a means of dealing with resistance to gender studies and feminist theory, as well as creating a consciousness-changing experience for the participants. The study is based on the documentation of courses I taught in three higher education institutions between 2012 and 2019: The Kibbutzim College of Education, Technology and the Arts and the Academic College of Society and the Arts, both in Israel, and the UN's University for Peace in Costa Rica. In addition, the educational practice was used in international trainings for peace and development workers from various international development agencies. Throughout the chapter, I will discuss examples of the objects presented by the students and the discourses generated by these presentations. These examples will form the basis for my analysis of how the objects were analyzed, regarding the material, social, and symbolic qualities they hold. Deconstructing and restructuring them allows for the implementation of wide critical gender observation skills and can bring about a significant change in consciousness among the learning community.

I will argue that using a gender-oriented analysis of everyday objects promotes understanding from a gender perspective of real-life situations and their influence on men, women, and people who do not identify by binary gender while focusing maximal attention on cultural differences and intersectionality. The chapter is structured according to the course learning process, beginning by briefly discussing the changing status of academic gender studies and the special challenges posed by these changes to students in compulsory courses and development organization training courses that include a compulsory module on gender. I will present the theoretical framework of working with everyday objects and discuss how it enables the lecturer to handle resistance and support a meaningful learning process, using some of the main themes that emerged in the courses and occupied the students: the beauty myth and body image, models of femininity and masculinity, and sexual violence. I will describe the dilemmas and conflicts arising from issues of feminism and academic language and specify the dynamics that promote multiculturalism in learning groups. I will demonstrate how the methodology promotes the creation of a safe space and solidarity within learning groups, and supports the sustainment of a positive, fruitful, and dialogical relationship between the lecturer and the students.

Gender in the academic (and development and peace work) field

Elective courses in gender studies have been offered in institutions of higher education since the 1990s (Herzog, 2009). Over the last decade, following the efforts of local feminist organizations in the public and legal spheres and in response to the international pressure regarding the UN Security Council Resolutions 1325 and 1820 to increase women's participation in decision-making processes, gender-oriented perspectives have been implemented in different spheres. For example, courses and continuing education programs on gender issues have become compulsory in some training programs for education workers, social workers, therapists, and workers in international peace and development organizations. At the same time, a change has taken place in gender studies programs. From programs intended mostly for upper-middle-class women already committed to the subject, imparting broad general knowledge on feminist issues and an aspiration to learn and deepen this knowledge, gender studies programs evolved into courses available to the public at large. This change was driven by the growing perception that gender-oriented perspectives should be assimilated in all aspects of life and "Feminism Is for Everybody" (hooks, 2000b). Turning to new "unnatural" and wider audiences presents a promising opportunity to deepen the social effect of gender studies programs. However, it requires rethinking and refreshing pedagogical tools to support the political and social change promoted by these programs. For example, the comprehensive emphasis on reading articles in English, a foreign language for the vast majority of students, may hinder the learning processes of new target audiences and impair the pedagogical, political, and social aims of the programs. Embracing the perceptions and methodology offered by feminist pedagogy can aid the formation of joint knowledge, as can studying and critically reading existing knowledge (Hird, 1998, 517–527).

Critical feminist pedagogy maps and analyzes the power structures in society with recourse to cultural and financial capital and hegemonic power possessed by different groups in the current social order (Saroyan & Amundsen, 2004). It creates awareness of the power distribution in society and manifestations of inequality in education with a critical approach, disassembling power relations in and out of the classroom, and via constant dialogue between the lecturer and the students. Questions of power, dominance, and related interactions are addressed in the learning group. Critical feminist pedagogy strives to make a change in society by presenting critical theories and translating them into emancipatory educational practices that examine the implications of identity—personal, collective, ethnic, racial, gender, and sexual orientation—in terms of access to various spheres of power. It further promotes understanding of social power relations and the ability to reflect on them as products of the everyday practices in which we engage (such as division of labor or tracking in the education system). Awareness of social structures and their reproduction develops an understanding of one's place in the world and the ability to mold and change it. Education is praxis; that is, theory and action in combination. The learning process is not strictly academic and theoretical, but also relates to everyday life. Changing the acceptable relationship between theory and practice and challenging the existent hierarchies of knowledge affects not only the content being taught but also the educational methods we use (McClure 2000, 53–55).

Feminist critical pedagogy addresses education while handling resistance as a means to structuring identity by viewing reality through a critical lens. Joint learning, and a raised awareness of political and social issues, generates an identical, cultural, and political narrative within a learning group that allows for a different and reflexive understanding of the world, how we operate in it, and the forms of reproduction and resistance available to us. Gender studies at its core is built on the recognition that gender is a relevant theory for analyzing reality (Butler & Scott, 1992) and that gender power relations must be recognized and altered. Feminist critical pedagogy suggests social change can be promoted by learning about the production and reproduction of the social structure mechanisms that preserve financial and cultural capital for certain groups (Saroyan & Amundsen, 2004). Studying enables learners to observe how they and the social contexts in which they are rooted are formed by power relations. Analyzing these enables the weaving of a historical narrative that validates and interprets personal experiences (such as sexual violence), employing these to inspire counter-action. The analysis also reflects on practices that reproduce certain power relations in everyday life (for example in the gender-based division of domestic tasks). At their best, gender studies courses move beyond the boundaries of traditional academic classes and become courses in "practical gender," meaning the direct application of gender theories to the students' everyday activities. Such courses promote viewing reality from a gendered perspective that is not focused on the difference between the sexes but on how society constructs power relations based on them. Gender analysis maps the manner in which this situation affects people of various genders in different ways, in terms of access to financial, social, and cultural resources, social and domestic roles, responsibilities both in the home and in the workplace, positions of prestige as well as elected posts, participation in decision-making systems, and power relations derived from legal and economic privileges and social structuring. Gender analysis offers a wider and clearer picture of people's needs in the light of their layered, complex, and intersectional identities (Crenshaw, 1991).

"The personal is political," one of the key slogans of the second wave of the feminist movement, is validated by gender studies. Several articles have already pointed out that gender studies have a profound effect on students, their paths through life, and their personal and professional interactions (Craig, 1992; Katz, 1999). For a considerable number of the learners, gender studies courses raise questions about their genders and sexual identities, as well as significant life choices such as relationships, family and parenthood. How these questions manifest can depend on one's social group and culture, class and/or life opportunities. For many women suffering intersectional oppression or discrimination and exploitation in various areas of their lives, the encounter with academic gender studies is also an encounter with the power fields that take part in forcing oppressive cultural and social norms.

Feminist critical pedagogy framework conceives of learning as a collaborative process between the lecturer and the student's personal life experiences while frequently pointing to the power relations in and out of the classroom. The classroom forms a space, a microcosm of social relations in which complex and sometimes painful issues in gender studies can be safely examined in a critical manner. One of the lecturer's roles in this context is to assist the students to share personal experiences, place them within a political and theoretical framework, and mirror to the learners how power relations based on class, ethnicity, race, religion, gender, and sexual preference are manifested in class. This offers the students a critical model they can adopt, as they do, both in classroom discussions and in their everyday lives (Banks, 1995; & Finkel, 1995). Critical pedagogy is oriented to social and political justice. The pedagogic approach suggests that raising students' awareness is a means for political and social change, and that it is raised by using relevant material and content from the learners' world (Slater, Fain, & Rossatto, 2002).

The goal of learning is to refine the learners' ability to think with a critical view of reality, to doubt, to ask questions, and develop an empowering consciousness of their subjective position. At the same time, critical pedagogy is meant to develop the learners' love of knowledge and their natural curiosity, often oppressed by society's view of underprivileged groups—typically the lower classes, racial and ethnic minorities, and women—as intellectually inferior. In other words, learning itself is intended to be an empowering experience. It affirms the value of the knowledge the learner already has, as well as her own value as an intellectual and theorist able to sustain a dialogue from a powerful position with the current (often non-inclusive and hegemonic) bodies of knowledge (Giroux, 1983; Luke & Gore, 1992). The lecturer's part in this process is to expose oppressive mechanisms and reassemble critical awareness and pedagogical alternatives (Giroux, 1988; Zalmanson-Levi, 2004; Darder, 2015). Most important, the lecturer must create a safe critical space that allows each student to undergo a personal process.

Gender analysis based on the relevance of everyday objects

Objects unveil a great deal about culture and identity and suggest unwritten narratives of social and political conflict (De Visser, 2006). The feminist scholar Adrienne Rich invites us to see, look at, and re-examine the current reality and to suggest new interpretations. Further dimensions of reality are revealed to us as we consider the part our own identities play in this examination (Rich, 1973). Sociologist Ervin Goffman suggests analyzing the symbolic meanings in images of objects within the context of gender identity structuring, where men are in control, active in the world, and play a central role in culture, while women are left on the margins of culture and society, often serving a decorative purpose (Goffman, 1956).

During the course, the students were asked to perform gender analysis on an object from their everyday life and to present the object and the analysis in class. The object might be a tool, a spiritual object, a luxury item, an object of sentimental value, and so on. The personal connection to the subject allows a gradual assimilation of gender perspective and thus a shift in consciousness. The object, any artifact from any field of life chosen by the student, is subject to a series of questions: How is the object used and by whom? Who manufactures it? How is it marketed and sold? Who is it intended for (explicitly and implicitly)? Who is allowed—and not allowed—to use it? What images and symbols are associated with the object? Which power relations does it embody? How does it reflect accessibility to resources, cultural or religious standpoints, group inclusion or exclusion? Is it private or public property? What are the various ownership relations pertaining to the object? (Evans, 1980; Giroux, 1983; hooks, 2000b). The students are specifically directed to examine how the object they chose affects men, non-binary, and women differently, and how it is influenced by men and women or femininity and masculinity; how the object participates in the relationship between gender and sexuality and how it symbolically reflects them. The place of the object in the world and of the world in the object makes room for critical analysis of power relations. Throughout their task, the students start to notice hegemonic mechanisms and power relations in many aspects of life and connect them to the lives they lead and to their own identity. The students were asked to present an object they believe reflects something from the culture or social world they come from. The term "culture" is not taken for granted but researched and applied in relation to local and ethnic traditions and global popular culture such as commercials.

When presenting the object, the student can "bring something of herself" to the classroom, literally or metaphorically. For students accustomed to having someone more qualified talk about the world and about themselves, this in itself is a substantial—if challenging—learning experience. Analyzing everyday objects allows the learners to tell their life stories themselves, as they choose to present them, and gives them a clear voice as subjects analyzing a relationship with an object. This exercise promotes analytical abilities with the interpretive freedom to feel confident in developing them. Integrating one's personal identity develops reflexive knowledge: What is my place in the world and why? Is this place fixed or changeable? What is it influenced by? The method also promotes critical and empowering observations on subjective structuring processes (Mohanty, 1988).

The reflexive aspect of the learning process requires particular consideration. Elizabeth Minnich (1988) defines reflexivity as a practice of examining our set of moral and cultural beliefs and scaling advantages, disadvantages, and implications from various and multidisciplinary perspectives. The reflexive position is the key to social change because it is based on the understanding that attitudes and values are contingent, historical, and cultural, and are bound to power relations. Attitudes and values can evolve, but a truly radical shift requires the agents of this change to critically examine their own premises. Students learn to doubt even what they perceive as obvious or absolute truth, and to notice how attitudes and values can be embodied in the physical material. Shifting one's focus to how both knowledge and facts are manufactured by assembling discourse and fields of practice calls for rethinking and discussing the politics of knowledge. The class learns to imagine the social and political consequences of different forms of knowledge of the world by creating their own gender studies learning and teaching materials (Freire & Macedo, 1987), examining the truths offered by different versions of knowledge, and evaluating whether the suggested world of knowledge is desirable or worthwhile. In other words, the class learns to view knowledge not as a series of mere logical procedures but to observe how knowledge touches the body, the emotions, the private and the public, the material and spiritual. As mentioned earlier, integrating diverse points of view and perceiving knowledge as a process originating from different theoretical and practical sources undermines the perception that knowledge itself is an artifact or an object that can be possessed once and for all. Knowledge, knowing, and learning are profoundly understood as an ongoing call for a dialogue (Minnich, 1988).

Handling resistance with feminist critical pedagogy practices

The courses I discuss in this chapter were originally designed as "classic" gender and women's studies courses, meaning a curriculum based on differentiating sex from gender as a collection of social structuring notions and reviewing the various waves of the feminist movement, with a focus on body and sexuality politics and layered, complex identities. The reading list I prepared included central and fundamental theories of gender inequality in culture and public institutions, theories regarding the construction of feminine and masculine identity, layered and intersectional identities, the representation of men and women in the media, economy, government, and politics, and the beauty ideal. It was designed to provide the students, most of whom were unacquainted with feminist theory, with a broad and multicultural perspective on the various ideologies in the movement. But my academic plans hit a wall of resistance as of the first lesson. The students objected to the academic language used in many of the articles (generating the feeling of being belittled and excluded), and also to feminist positions perceived in the public sphere as anti-feminine (suggesting the expectation that one detach oneself from the hegemonic culture and the beauty ideal in particular).

"I came to this course loaded with resistance, I didn't want to study gender but it is mandatory," is a sentence I hear at the beginning of each of my gender courses. The courses trigger strong resistance and emotions on three levels. The first concerns the very idea of studying a subject that questions social structuring and undermines the obvious regarding the learner's identity, social class, and social position. The second is a profound resistance to academic and theoretical jargon, the latter being associated with hegemonic power of a certain cultural capital and perceived by the students as foreign and alienating. The third level concerns perceptions of feminism, especially regarding the beauty myth; students criticize what they refer to as "the beauty and slimming industry." At the same time, however, the students make statements such as "I don't want to look like an ill-groomed feminist after the course," suggesting a perception of feminists as women who deliberately wish to look ill-groomed in order to "prove a point."

At the beginning of the semester, many of the students' views on gender and feminism are saturated in stereotypes, and they often claim that gender studies are "not for them" because they are not feminists. Friedman (1999) presents stereotypical perceptions of feminism held by many women and even by activists for gender equality. Her research shows that many women perceive feminism as threatening, aggressive, and extreme, and therefore as an ideology or practice that does not represent them. Others perceive feminism as a movement for white upper-class women with whom they do not identify (Abu-Baker, 2007). The students often describe experiences in which feminist lecturers have behaved in a judgmental and conflictual manner, blaming the students for internalizing oppression and being unaware of the discrimination against them. Some students raised concerns that the course might destroy their motivation to be pretty and feminine, leaving them angry and bitter (Wolf, 1990). In many cases, a gender analysis of everyday objects bridges gender, feminism, and everyday life in such a way that these students began to speak of a "connection" with the subject.

The statement "I won't learn from you" or simply "not learning" is analyzed by Kohl (1999) as a political act of resistance to learning and deepening knowledge that can undermine the student's identity. Kohl defines refusing to learn as a political act that can be altered by a political reading of an act or a behavior and a relevant profound connection of the learners to the study materials. Kohl claims that recognizing this is a necessary step in working with resistance that helps to expose the mechanisms of political, economic, and symbolic power that operates on all levels of the education system and throughout society. Students who can identify with their own language, culture, religion, and the identities that intersect with those elements will do better in their studies and contribute to the group process. Students who refrain from bringing materials to the classroom that represent their ethnic, racial, gender, and class identity might feel out of place, actively resist, and even drop out (Zinn, 1974; Gates, 1986; Ayers, 1995; Cleaver & Cleaver, 2006).

Freire and Shor, in their well-known book *Pedagogy of Liberation* (1987), discuss in detail the subject of resistance in education and offer a number of strategies. Shor stresses the importance of dialogue with his students:

> Dialogue must be understood as something taking part in the very historical nature of human beings. It is part of our historical progress in becoming human beings. That is, a dialogue is a kind of necessary posture to the extent that humans have become more and more critically communicative beings. Dialogue is a moment where humans meet to reflect on the reality as they make and remake it.
>
> (Freire & Shor, 1987, 98)

One method of overcoming resistance is to design the lesson together. This challenges the traditional power relations between lecturer and students, reconstructing learning as an act of sharing and mutual recognition in the equally valuable, if different, contributions that every participant brings to the group. Constructing the curricula and the specific lessons around the students' knowledge of the world and the subjects relevant to their lives is an integral part of this process. Addressing resistance is not meant to make it "disappear"; on the contrary, in critical pedagogy, learners' resistance is of political value and meaning—whether conscious or unconscious—to the student. Discussing resistance creates an opportunity for empowering dialogue and learning while giving the students and their knowledge of the world a voice (Freire, 1976). While their voice is heard throughout the course in the way they express themselves in their own spoken language, dealing with other languages such as academic English or other languages associated with social power and exclusion is part of the course's learning process (Freire, Freire, & de Oliveira, 2014).

One of the first examples of class and gender analysis in the course was the language in which the articles are written. During my courses, I often meet students who are threatened by the concept of academic learning and display a profound resistance to the unfamiliar academic language. They describe dealing with articles and material that are supposed to represent them and their lives as detracting, alienating, and belittling. The very existence of those feelings and the willingness to openly discuss them in class in a respectful and serious manner opens the door to an enabling educational dialogue. The students' feelings are recognized, and they learn that the differentiation between "feelings" and "thoughts" is historical and political, and itself reflects settled power relation with gender aspects.

In response to the students' resistance to the academic language, we offer a critical analysis, inquiring as to who benefits and who loses from using it: What power relations are promoted and reproduced by academic language? And in what power fields is it rooted? Exploring power relations and the term "hegemony" led students to organize study groups focused on "translating" the academic texts into clearer language, while studying the sociological and gender-based jargon and concepts out of a deliberate and political intention to take part in the academic discourse (Newberry, Gallant, & Riley, 2013). At the same time, I assist in clarifying the central arguments and theoretical contexts of the texts studied by writing every new term on the board and translating it into accessible everyday language. This formed trust and enabled a smoother entry into the world of gender studies.

Academic writing that describes and analyzes phenomena such as racism, ethnicity, and class and their intersections with gender, religion, and geographic location offers a theoretical and intellectual framework in which students can confront the worlds in which they live; however, the way in which many academic texts are written causes many of them to feel alienated and out of place, along with difficulties in understanding the academic materials and a sense of failure. Discussing the politics of language allows the student to place herself as the critic and analyst, and not only a passive subject to the analysis of the symbolic social power holders. This is the path from resistance to empowering discourse (Mackie, 1980). The principles of feminist critical pedagogy were expressed in the construction of the lessons. In each lesson, a student was to present a gender analysis of her everyday object, a process that undermines the hierarchical order subordinating the learner to the closed and dominant knowledge possessed by the lecturer. Since the students presented an object they are familiar with and rooted in their unique worlds, the lecturer became part of the learning group, turning the learning process into a more collaborative one. The main learning methodology is an open discussion guided by the lecturer with the students' participation; all present pay attention and use clear language. Questions and clarifications are accepted at any stage of the discussion, and every unclear term is written on the board and clarified by the group (Giroux, 1983; Luke & Gore, 1992).

A large part of resistance to studying gender-related materials is grounded in negative stereotypes of the feminist movement and feminist women. A prominent concern raised by the students was that a feminist discourse that highlights power relations will be in essence a violent aggressive discourse that promotes "hating men", a discourse that might antagonize them towards what they consider to be feminine and destroy the beauty model to which they are accustomed. Analyzing an object that is related to a discourse about the body and the beauty industry usually opens the course, opening a discussion on the divisions between masculine and feminine, beauty and ugliness, and what political meanings are hidden in the beauty and cosmetic industry. For many women, choosing to present an object from the beauty industry, for example a beauty or skincare product they use, is an act of resistance since they assume feminists are not pretty or well-groomed. Sun,[1] a Japanese student at the UN's University of Peace, presented skin-whitening creams which are common in Japanese consumer culture. Using images from commercials, newspapers, fashion photography, and traditional Japanese art she demonstrated how the Japanese perception of beauty perceives white skin as beautiful, correct, attractive, pure, and clean, and dark skin as inferior, ugly, shameful, and in need of creams to whiten it. In this course, half of the learning group was of Asian origin and the discussion revolved around the effectiveness of the cream and the levels of skin whitening possible. The connection between ethics, aesthetics, and skin whiteness was not challenged. I therefore concluded that, at that point in time, the critical approach was too intense, the discussion reflecting the common view with no reflection or criticism.

One important question at this stage is how, if at all, the lecturer should point out the hegemonic processes that mold the obvious social and cultural connection between skin color, gender, and the beauty myth. I decided, at this stage of the course, to present the development of body and beauty perceptions worldwide to the students while discussing key theories on the subject. For example, *Black Skin, White Masks* by Frantz Fanon (1967) was discussed in a dialogue with Naomi Wolf's *The Beauty Myth*, suggesting a meeting between worlds and texts that encourage critical questioning about economy, culture, globalization, ethics, and aesthetics. The fact that the lesson was focused on Western beauty perceptions allowed the conversation in class to move away from specific criticism of Asian culture in a way that allowed Sun to remain open-minded and draw conclusions about her own culture from learning about Europe and North America. The conversation around the beauty myth and its connection to power relations in the West created an opportunity to present objects related to the cosmetic and beauty industry in the east without direct criticism, and led to a series of presentations of various beauty products by East Asian students. Reading selected parts of Wolf's *The Beauty Myth* created a discourse acknowledging that different cultures operate different mechanisms that are identical in their motives and methods regarding women. Such mechanisms produce a beauty ideal that financially, physically, and mentally enslaves women, working hand in hand with other socialization, exploitation, and subordination mechanisms. This has paved the way to certain norms in different cultures, such as hair dying or wearing high heels as a professional demand, strict dress codes, body hair removal, and makeup. The conversation in class focused on the differences in how these norms are applied and enforced on both men and women, and the sanctions on each gender. This raised questions on femininity, power, and beauty, and led to anger, criticism, and doubt on the part of the students regarding the transparency of those mechanisms to them. The wall of resistance was cracked and opened up the possibility to discuss the beauty industry in the context of body image and constructions of femininity and masculinity.

Femininities and masculinities

The question of whether the differences between women and men are biological or that gender is not necessarily bound to biological sex is frequently raised by students. Many of them begin by arguing that there are biological differences between females and males, such as strength and women's ability to give birth. Classic feminist theories (de Beauvoir, Paul, Wolf, Steinham) are new to a large number of students, and the perception that there is a fundamental difference between sex and gender is surprising and confusing. The more they link feminist criticism to characteristics they perceive as masculine or feminine, the more they point out that these phenomena—discrimination, oppression, exploitation, a clear division into gender roles, and more—were relevant to their grandmothers and mothers, and today they have faded somewhat. Many students purport that dealing with social structures of the past actually damages women who are perceived by society as inferior to men. Female students voice their concern that merely discussing different perceptions of femininity and masculinity will engender inequality.

Through a gender analysis of objects, a wide variety of body gestures, styles of clothing, hobbies, occupations, and behaviors with a negative or positive charge, active or passive, feminine or masculine are discussed in class. This variety lays out the possibilities of choosing or not choosing actions that are tied to the structuring of femininity or masculinity. The main insight that emerges in class from this process is that the accepted distinctions between women and men are deceptive; a range of behaviors and gestures reflect both genders. We discuss the fundamental differences between biological sex and social structures and how we are all "gendered" (Butler 1993). For example, in one of the first lessons at the University for Peace in Costa Rica, Christa presented razor blades designed for men and women. She showed, among other things, that razors are designed, planned, and manufactured in the same way, the only difference between them being the color of the plastic and the cost, which is about 30 percent higher for women's razors (the so-called "pink tax").

Dialogue, and critical questions about the objects they present, leads the students to the understanding that "becoming a woman" implies a profound process of socialization; that there is no "natural" feminine behavior and no "real" masculine behavior, but a socially structured range of gestures, symbols, use of language and other practices that shape masculinity and femininity as cultural and discursive performance. The students put into writing their questions and dilemmas about biological difference versus social structuring and examine these against the reality of their lives. They inquire as to what "natural" resistance is and what stems from a social-historical power structure. This creates a complex picture. On the one hand, the students claim that many of their behaviors are "natural" and "innate," and on the other they choose a different behavior that is not dictated to them. At the same time, we map and classify behaviors that are considered masculine and classify them according to accepted social values: high/low and positive/negative. Among other things, they present walking, sitting, and standing in a "masculine" and "feminine" way, examining, among other things, the social structuring acquired through observing others, imitation, and cultural messages from photographs and advertisements (Goffman, 1956). The mapping process sharpens their understanding that most of the characteristics defined by the students as positives are perceived by them as masculine characteristics and what they define as female characteristics are seen as negative.

Following the discussion on how social structuring creates masculine or feminine behavior that can be perceived as negative or positive depending on the culture, the time, and place, Odette, a French-American student employed in international organizations, chose smoking cigarettes as a gendered practice in different parts of the world. Odette's analysis, based on her life experiences, related to the way men and women perceived her as a smoker in different places and contexts. She presented nine brief situations in different parts of the world (India,

Colombia, Peru, Ecuador, Costa Rica, Democratic Republic of the Congo). On the one hand, she felt perceived variously as a permissive woman, sometimes seductive, or even as a prostitute or as a woman who allows herself to be seen as such. On the other hand, she felt that smoking lent her the image of a masculine, powerful, and aggressive woman, or a respectable older woman. Odette compared this dichotomy of the smoking woman to the male smoking culture in the same places. "In indigenous communities in Ecuador, I walked for hours to distant communities, and the people around me connected my smoking to power, and I felt that they saw me as a stranger and as masculine and also as an old woman because only old women smoke." Odette's encounters and interactions with different cultures in the world once again emphasize the different cultural patterns of femininity, and at the same time raise the issue of the privileges of the European woman, whose smoking may be tolerated in places where smoking is considered forbidden for local women. At the end of the analysis, Odette shared with the group another dimension of smoking as a gendered phenomenon: She said that her partner stopped smoking as a signal to her that it was time she became pregnant.

Odette analyzed an object that constituted a recurring motif throughout her life. The daily, almost obvious motif enabled her to examine smoking from a critical and complex perspective that takes into account the gender aspects of structuring femininity and masculinity in cultural, class, economic, and physical contexts, paying close attention to how they affect the environment. She dealt with how the environment structured her feminine-Western identity facing the ethno-cultural and class-based "other" (Shochat 2001). Odette ended her presentation by saying that the environment, culture, and the transition between cultures have established the (feminine) woman she is today. She added that, following the critical point of view acquired during the course, she had decided to give up smoking. Odette spoke of how, as a smoker, she was supporting the exploitative processes of tobacco companies that enslave, humiliate, and impoverish women at the levels of production, advertising, and marketing, alongside the more severe health consequences associated with smoking as a woman. The discussion revolved around the connection between the way smoking is perceived in different parts of the world for different genders and that smoking as a practice and cigarettes as a product are perceived in a completely different manner based on gender, class, age, and personal status. The lack of debate about smoking among older men was related to the concept of "transparency" and social structures of masculinity. The way a man who smokes is perceived positively as "normal" and "ordinary," while a smoking woman is perceived as negative, different, permissive, or sexy. The social structuring of smoking women requires special attention—and became an example for gender power relations in the course. Students who firmly argued that inequality is largely based on biological differences and that, in their country, there is gender equality now perceived social structuring in terms of the price women pay, for example, for smoking in public, for broader mechanisms of oppression and discrimination. This reflective action in the learning group was received with enthusiastic applause. The students commented that the personal exposure connected them to the subject and made them think about how their own identities are structured in relation to the place or places where they grew up.

Power relations, objectification and reclaiming

Power relations and the issue of "objectification" arise regularly in the students' presentations. Understanding and recognizing the objectification of the female body (that is, the transformation of the female body into commodity and object, and comparison of women to objects and property) is introduced gradually in the course in order to avoid resistance. The realization that gender power relations exist in society and the awareness that almost all women in class had felt objectified at some point in their lives generated a discourse of female solidarity and astonishment inflamed with anger and self-doubt: how could we not see these mechanisms of power and objectification to which we were subjected? The gender analysis at this stage of the course focuses on objects; comparing objects to women and men; object–subject relations; rereading of ownership relations; and reclaiming objectification (Redfern 2013).

Lina, a Swiss student who took part in a master's degree course in gender at the Department of Media of the UN's University for Peace, presented a Swiss watch and examined how this product affects, and is affected by, power relations between men and women. She focused on analyzing the product's instruction manual and advertisements for watches designed for women and men. She demonstrated, among other things, that watches marketed to men transmit power, prestige, and status. The advertisements for these watches display all the clock's technological functions, even if, as Lina rightfully wondered, it is unclear how many of the men who wear a Rolex use it to navigate or to measure air pressure in the depths of the ocean. On the other hand, parallel "feminine" watches were presented as jewelry that women receive mainly from the men who are courting them. The gender analysis of the watch advertisements focused on the watch's appearance and sexual symbolism. Lina argued that women who wear a Swiss watch that cost tens of thousands of dollars radiate not their own power but the power of the man from whom they received it. The women in those advertisements seem unusually happy; some appear to be receiving a gift or an engagement present, and most of them are semi-naked, wearing a gold watch and diamonds as a prestigious status symbol. This connects the watch and the woman as masculine status symbols. According to Lina's analysis, the advertising targets men as the audience for both men's and women's watches. The imagined woman in the advertisement is supposed to be impressed by the male watch or devote herself to a man who gives her a feminine watch that represents his power and his economic and social status. "The watch" was conceptualized in class to describe the cases in which women represent an object bought by men to glorify themselves and represent their social and economic power. Following the gender analysis of the Swiss watch, women in the class raised questions and dilemmas about accepting gifts and object–subject relations in an intimate relationship. Many wore a watch or another piece of jewelry that represented to them their partner's economic and social value. They commented that in North America the cost of an engagement ring is equivalent to a full monthly wage of the future spouse and is supposed to reflect his economic power that will be given to "his woman." Students presented examples from around the world of cultural perceptions centralizing size and economic value, and hence the social status of cars, apartments, dresses, and jewelry, and raised questions about the status of relationships and love in light of power and property relations. In general, social structuring, hierarchical gender perceptions, objectification, and subject–object relations are complex teaching and learning subjects for a course in gender because these subjects make the theoretical and political personal. Mediating the theories through practices of feminist critical pedagogy, analyzing objects that are relevant to the students, refines the feminist argument regarding objectification using examples brought by the students. The learning process is based on changing the attitudes towards, and reflection on, these objects.

Lina's cultural context (Switzerland) opened up an intense discussion about how worthwhile it can be to reveal to "others," people who do not share the same culture, the deficiencies, and inequalities that objects from different parts of the world represent. The students raised dilemmas about exposing inequality, which was linked to broader questions addressed in the course: the "transparency" (or lack of) of power relations, oppressive mechanisms, and perceptions of how different cultures treat women, which can often be thoroughly challenged when multicultural work is based on personal narratives and life stories. During the work on gender analysis of everyday objects, the students' narratives clearly show that the mechanisms in different places around the world are similar, albeit different daily realities. A seemingly simple matter of "airing one's dirty laundry in public" has become a critical discussion about the concealment and exposure of mechanisms that preserve the existing gender status quo. Some cultures often perceive exposing mechanisms of oppression as a betrayal of their culture, nationality, or religion, such as Asian and African students I spoke with at the UN University for Peace, or Palestinian citizens of Israel in Jewish-Israeli academia. As a minority group within a hegemonic culture, they feel that they must positively represent the place they came from. They often mentioned in class that when they could speak their language or relate to elements of their culture in a way that was not perceived as "special" or "exotic" it would be easier for them to speak about their experiences of gender discrimination (Brooking, Foster, Smith, & Runnymede Trust 1987; Kaplan & Miller 2007; Sleeter & Grant 2007).

In the same course, Rah, a student from Cambodia, introduced women's sexual objectification through the simple act of eating a banana. Rah opened the presentation of his object with an act that could be seen as "reclaiming"; he handed each student a banana in its skin and asked them to eat it (White, White, & Korgen 2014). He said that, in Cambodia, men pick, peel, and eat a banana directly from the tree, while women will be considered promiscuous if they do likewise. Women will generally pick the banana and not peel it until they are at home and have cut the banana into small pieces with a knife and fork. The phallic connotations of bananas prevent Cambodian women from eating them in public. This and other similar presentations inspired discussion on how women are expected to eat and the sexual connotations that the masculine objectifying gaze might associate with this act. When a man smokes a cigarette, uses a fork, or eats a banana, it is considered normal, socially transparent. However, when women smoke or eat, especially in the public sphere, it has far-reaching social implications that are not directly related to their biological sex.

Relationships, love, and sisterhood

The students also analyzed everyday objects symbolizing love and relationships. They examined commercial representations of love, such as balloons, roses, and chocolate given to women on Valentine's Day, the gender-related division of labor between spouses, the use of contraception, and rituals such as engagement and marriage. For many of the students, relationships and love represented a conflict with the theories of power property relations addressed in the course; the dilemmas were discussed openly with the support of the women's group formed during the course.

Shirley, a Danish student at the University of Peace in Costa Rica, showed YouTube videos of marriage proposals around the world, where a man gives a woman a very expensive ring and "becomes his." She analyzed this ritual as a promise of masculine economic and physical protection and "marking" the woman as traditionally entering the tribe of the man. The marriage proposal itself is perceived as a proactive action, and therefore masculine, and the woman can passively accept or, not in all cultures, refuse, the proposal. For men, entering into marriage is a commitment to protect and provide for the woman and the family unit. On her part, the woman guarantees loyalty, support, love, and family. "Taking a woman's hand," Shirley continued, means, in other words, accepting the services that this hand can carry out. Shirley analyzed the way in which she herself had proposed marriage to her partner and wondered whether she might have put her wife in an uncomfortable position when she asked for her hand in front of the whole family. Did the spouse actually have the option of refusing? Did it involve power relations? Can women apply patriarchal oppressive mechanisms and is exploitation of power in a marriage proposal always negative? Can marriage be a feminist act? What do "feminists" have to say about love and relationships? Questions and presentation requests about feminist theories discussing monogamy versus polyamory and open marriage rendered the lesson more attractive and stimulating for students who shared their life experiences with the learning group. The students compared the institution of marriage to that of academia in terms of the lesson structure, arguing that just as it is possible to teach in a non-hierarchical way, it is also possible to maintain a relationship built on equity. The groups conducted an intersectional analysis, that in this practice includes economic analysis, to marriage and discovered that men tend to earn more after they marry as the workplace perceives them as more stable and in need for a permanent position as providers. Women, on the other hand, tend to earn less and will be encouraged by many employers to reduce their responsibilities and hours and thus, tend to earn less.

In feminist critical pedagogy, practices that break down the power relations between learners and teachers are created on the basis of appreciation and the desire to learn. Such practices fall under the broad definition of dialog and empowerment. The dialog in critical pedagogy is an educational, political, and ideological tool that creates a bond of reciprocity, love, and solidarity between the teacher and the learners (Freire, 1972). The lecturer studies the students' world with them through dialogue and by sharing varied types of knowledge (Zalmanson-Levi, 2012; Freire & Shor, 1990). Dialogue and empowerment throughout the course are multidimensional and multi-directional. The open and nonjudgmental discourse, together with the opportunity to present a gender analysis of objects from their lives and thereby bring their own voices, opinions, and dilemmas into the classroom, creates a network of women (and men) who support, consult, receive, and offer to help one another. This network creates an empowering feminist solidarity that shifts the boundaries of academic discourse and the daily reality of the students (hooks 2000c).

Sexuality and rape culture

According to the data provided by the World Health Organization, one out of every three women in the world has been sexually assaulted, and one out of everyone—all women—has experienced sexual harassment. The #MeToo and #WhyIDidntReport campaigns highlight how "rape culture" is present in the everyday reality of women from all layers of society and most cultures and shed light on sexual misconduct also within academia, peace organizations, major development agencies, and the UN. Naturally, this subject occupies the students in the compulsory course in gender studies. The discussions around the body as object, body image, and relationships between genders have transformed the subjects of sexual abuse, harassment, rape, and rape culture into central issues. In the first few weeks of the course, some students left the class when the subject of rape was mentioned or when a student presented an analysis that referred to sexual assault. Later, more and more students shared personal stories, often accompanied by self-blame. On the basis of the trust and support built within the group over time and the visibility of the discourse around "rape culture" in social media and the wider culture, the students were increasingly able to critically discuss the mechanisms of victim-blaming and spoke of exposing sexual assault as a tool for personal empowerment and a change in consciousness, as well as for solidarity and sisterhood among students.

At the Academic College of Society and Arts, Ravit, a student working as a waitress in a bar, presented a gender analysis of the glasses in which the various drinks were served and analyzed the fact that many men wanted to replace the cocktail glass so as not to be perceived by their friends as feminine. The presentation gave rise to a discussion among a few students, all of whom worked as waitresses, who decided to conduct an experiment on Ravit's hypothesis in their various workplaces. This initiative led to further findings on the perceptions of femininity and masculinity in bars and restaurants: Which foods are eaten by hand or with cutlery? Which drinks are sucked through a straw? The students learned the term "male fragility" and used it often to describe men who refuse to hold what they consider a feminine glass or drink.

The questions were developed into mini-research on "rape culture" that asked: What dangers lurk for women from date-rape drugs in bars and clubs and what might be protective measures? In another lesson, one of the students introduced the symbolic process of rape. She analyzed how rape affects women and men differently, described the various kinds of social support available to rape survivors, and the social, medical, economic, and psychological costs for both men and women. She finished her presentation by saying that the analysis had taken her on an inner journey to dark, silenced places that now can "have air," and she can receive support and solidarity.

Kiyo-san, a Japanese student who took part in a compulsory gender course at the UN University in Costa Rica, began the course with a strong statement in front of the class: She spoke of her belief that all people are equal and that they have equal opportunities to work and realize their potential. In another lesson she claimed that body modification surgeries do not create a negative body image, but rather bring about happiness and increased self-esteem. Although she noted that it was difficult for her to deal with certain body issues, Kiyo-san asked me to present materials about women who had learned to "decide" about their own bodies themselves and rejected corporatized and commercialized control of their bodies. In this context, I introduced the class to the term "reclaiming" and the way activists redeem negative labeling into empowering language. We talked about the terms "feminist," "lesbian," and "witch" as examples of negative labels that can become a source of strength and power if we make them "ours." As a result of the gender analysis of rape, Kiyo-san raised a question about the possibility of reclaiming the raped body. The learning group carefully asked how these questions are related to the object she chose to present, which led to Kiyo-san sharing a difficult experience of sexual assault during an internship at a United Nations agency. The stories of sexual harassment and assault accumulated and the class conversation contributed towards a body of knowledge about sexual harassment and assaults in workplaces, academia and peace work, in the wake of the #MeToo campaign. We could see how the discourse on these topics transformed into a topic that is discussed and therefore also conceptualized, learned, and processed by the group and hopefully later by them as teachers, trainers, and peace workers.

Kyle (one of the students from Japan) brought a raincoat to analyze and said that while men use it to protect against the rain, she uses it in the subway to protect her clothes from "the outcome of public masturbation." She described a situation on cramped public transport where people stand very close to each other and some men take advantage of this and masturbate on their way to or from work. The group asked why she wouldn't vocally protest or hit back against her assaulter and Kyle explained that in this context she is ashamed, embarrassed, and therefore silenced. We linked her and other experiences to politics of silence and social network campaigns such as "breaking the silence #MeToo—why I didn't complain" campaign which provide support, theoretical, and context framework to survivors of sexual assault. It highlights that rape culture exists in nearly every country in the world. The mechanisms that maintain it, I claim, are silence and the notion that rape is a localized incident—we feel it only happened to "her," effectively clearing one of agency and responsibility. The campaigns that undercover the size and scope of the phenomenon raise awareness that almost every woman has experienced sexual harassment during her life, and that by raising our voices we may create defense mechanisms to protect women and men who are survivors of rape and sexual assault. Such consciousness-raising also goes some way to educating the public that rape culture exists, is morally reprehensible, and needs to be transformed by men and women. By challenging cultural norms, open discussion, and providing mutual protection, we may contest a woman's decision to wear a raincoat on the subway in the faith that others will be empowered to intervene and shame the sexual offender rather than the survivor. Silencing in society is further reflected as a widespread phenomenon of women and girls in the education system.

Kiyo-san presented a gender analysis of Bento boxes used by children to carry meals to school. The food is cut, prepared, and decorated in a highly aestheticized manner. According to Kiyo-san, in Japanese schools, there is an unwritten but implicit competition between schoolchildren as to who has the most beautiful Bento box: a reflection of the social status of women in society. The labor-intensive process of designing food as bears, flowers, and *anime* characters has been offered as a partial explanation as to why majority of Japanese women do not work outside the household (Inoue, Nishikitani, Tsurugano, 2016). Kiyo-san also linked the external image of the food box to that of women in Japanese society, and especially to the constant preoccupation with external beauty as symbolic of inner value. The value of women, she explained, was measured in their ability to decorate their children's food boxes while underscoring the difficulty and effort associated with this unremunerated labor. Kiyo-san compared the silence of the women regarding the competition between them over Bento boxes to the broader social demand of hiding the traumas associated with the female body. The hidden mechanisms that keep women in modern society at home are, according to Kiyo-san, the same mechanisms that preserve the conspiracy of silence regarding both sexual assault and the feminine role (as decorative) in society at large.

Kiyo-san explained that she had conducted a survey among her friends, which suggested that few women in higher education plan to marry because they wish to work outside the household. The class discourse on the social pressures faced by women to be beautiful and well groomed, while hiding the physical and emotional pain they experience, revealed to Kiyo-san the symbolic nature of Bento boxes as perfect feminine motherhood, decorating the world for children and men. Kiyo-san's gender analysis is illustrative of a broadened social consciousness created during the course; one that directly links the theory of gender, discrimination mechanisms, rape culture, the silencing and oppression of women, and everyday objects as symbolic of culture. The disclosure of Kiyo-san's own sexual assault brought about a fundamental change in the student and in the group as a whole. Questions about ways to regain control of the body and turn derogatory names and traumatic events into a source of power took on a different meaning in the context of the sexual assault.

Another example from Japan was given by Horimo, who spoke of how, in Japan, women dried their underwear inside the house in order to avoid its theft. Horimo explained that men buy used women's panties (laundered ones are cheaper) for sniffing; such products are called, in free translation, "women's panties for inhalation." Such used underwear can be purchased from vending machines at railway and bus stations and on street corners. Underwear is also often sold on the Internet by young girls, who can receive up to $500 for them. Here again, as the class discussed, female sexuality is objectified. However, Japanese students in the class who were embarrassed by the discussion stressed that not all Japanese men buy and "sniff" underwear. Comparing this practice to sex work for girls appeared unfounded to them. They explained that it is a social phenomenon resulting from men wishing to be perceived as consumers of pornography or other symbols of sexuality in the public space, and especially on crowded trains. This is, in other words, a phenomenon related to the production and representation of masculinity just as much as it relates to femininity. The group discussion following the presentation revolved around the relationship between the female body and the masculine gaze, the existence and shape of a woman's view of the woman's body, and the manner in which representations of the woman's body in different cultures are shaped within the framework of power relations, hegemony, and cultural symbol systems.

May, a student from Vietnam, presented a lubricating gel. She explained that with this object she hoped to address the pain that many women suffer during sex. During the presentation, she shared her embarrassment about using the lubricant and concluded by saying, "There's nothing to be done. For a relationship, you have to suffer some pain during sex." The other students applauded and cheered May for daring to share such an intimate and embarrassing subject; some classmates hugged her. In addition, a group of students insisted that sex should not hurt at all. We talked about the complexities of sex and about the awkwardness of discussing it, both with one's partner and with other people. We linked sex to critical and queer theories that undermine the notion that there is only one way—in essence heteronormative—to have sex. We also discussed the perception that sexual relations are defined by the penetration of a woman by a man. This concept received a mixed reception by the students, as liberating, funny, and yet embarrassing at the same time. One student volunteered to bring sex toys for women into the classroom that offer alternatives to penetration. As a result of our course, she later led a workshop and then a lecture on queer sex.

Conclusions

A large number of students shared difficult experiences of sexual harassment, assault, and rape in both the distant and recent past, which they were able to address with the solidarity and support of the group. Critical questions were voiced regarding the political structures that allow for control over women, especially those vulnerable to multiple discrimination because of their intersectional identities. At the same time, the group began to critically examine the possibility of sharing personal stories. What is the price of differential exposure imposed on women from different groups? To what extent is this kind of exposure a cultural function, and/or a privilege that not all women share?

This method of combining a critical scrutiny of society with and within a supportive group renders the subject of gender studies a unique experience for the students, especially those for whom this is the first encounter with the field. It is the finding of this methodology that women experience particular empowerment when sharing difficult and complex experiences; the objects and symbols associated with these, and reclaiming them: turning pain, shame, negative labeling, or trauma into sources of strength and power.

The examples discussed in this chapter show how students gradually acquire a broader perspective on gender and learned to translate common practices in their lives into the theoretical language required for the course. The encounter of the personal social and cultural world within the academic context generated a change in the student's consciousness that manifested both personally and collectively in the learners' group. This new encounter between theory and pedagogy is compelling and creates a new practice that may have important implications on the development of an academic field originally designed for feminist women (and perhaps a few men allies) into a subject studied in compulsory courses by much broader audiences. Gender and women's studies lecturers today face new and existing challenges concerning the theoretical and political achievements of the feminist movement for diverse groups. This opportunity highlights the lecturers' and scholars' commitment to learning through listening to their students. This new integration of practice and gender theory has the potential to advance gender studies into a theory that goes hand in hand—both politically and pedagogically—with practice.

In addition, active inclusion of the students in the learning process—the possibility to bring material they find interesting in relation to gender—assists in broadening the range of language and discourse used in the course. The learning process is thus not only based on a passive study of feminist theory but also on how it can be translated into everyday language. Precisely because this translation is never comprehensive or absolute, integrating academic language with spoken language gives voice to multiple points of view and interpretative options. The personal, cultural, and social perspectives of the students become a relevant source for understanding the world as legitimate gender theorists. Academic language gradually transforms from a foreign and alienating jargon to a challenge the students willingly accept.

This profound systemic integration of the students in the learning process brings about a shift in the traditional authoritative lecturer–student relationship. The lesson was largely based on the students' commitment to broadening the scope of discussion from their own personal and cultural worlds; they became the expert for the lecturer and the rest of the learning group. The course offers a safe space that enables both deliberation and active experimentation in new forms of human relationships: mutual respect, positive acceptance of authority, and rejection of authoritarian and oppressive practices.

For the students who claim at the beginning of the course that gender analysis is not relevant to the second decade of the twenty-first century, the course generates a change in consciousness thanks to the accumulation of experiences raised in class, the proposed analysis, and questions of femininity and distribution of labor in private and public contexts. Positions and patterns the students believe belonged to the past were suddenly made explicit in numerous contexts. Naturally, the students began to "see gender" everywhere, question and examine the relation between the personal and the political, and for many it resulted in feelings of anger, insult, and helplessness. However, the safe space of the course and the possibility to gently and respectfully analyze personal life experiences allowed the women to turn the surfaced facts on oppression into a source of power.

Many students give positive feedback about the course, describing it as one of the most central and meaningful courses in the degree curriculum, and some even as "life-changing." Students comment that they are no longer able to view reality without the lens of gender analysis. Many mention that they read all the items on the reading list, spend many hours in research and thought, and present their projects and the object to friends, family, and significant others. The final course paper requires the students to elaborate on their presentation in class; these papers exceed in terms of quality papers submitted to me in other courses, both in terms of the depth of the research and the level of scholarly analysis. This begs the question as to the long-term effects of compulsory courses in gender on students and the gender analysis assimilation in their educational and development and therapeutic work—a promising topic for future study.

The same practice has been introduced in gender training programs in addition to gender mainstreaming modules for politicians, diplomats, and civil servants, and has had a strong educational effect on their understanding of what gender analysis is and why is it important, in addition to a connection between personal experiences and the world knowledge needed to map and analyze a given situation.

Note

1 The names of all students mentioned in the text have been changed to protect the individuals' identity.

References

Abu-Baker, K. 2007. "Multiple Meanings of Feminism as an Example of Multi-Cultural Education: Feminism of Arab Women as a Case Study." In P. Peri (ed.), *Education in Multi-Cultural Society*, 187–209. Jerusalem: Carmel. (In Hebrew.)

Ayers, W. 1995. *To Become a Teacher: Making a Difference in Children's Lives*. New York: Teachers College Press.

Banks, J.A. & Banks, C.A.M. 1995. "Equity Pedagogy: An Essential Component of Multicultural Education." *Theory into Practice* 34(3): 152–158.

Bollin, G.G. & Finkel, J. 1995. "White Racial Identity as a Barrier to Understanding Diversity: A Study of Preservice Teachers." *Equity and Excellence* 28(1): 25–30.

Brooking, C., Foster, M., Smith, S., & Runnymede Trust. 1987. *Teaching for Equality: Educational Resources on Race and Gender*. London: Runnymede Trust.

Butler, J. 1993. *Bodies that Matter: On the Discursive Limits of "Sex."* New York: Routledge.

Butler, J. & Scott, J.W. 1992. *Feminists Theorize the Political*. New York: Routledge.

Cleaver, E. & Cleaver, K. 2006. *Target Zero: A Life in Writing*. New York: Palgrave Macmillan.
Craig, S. 1992. *Men, Masculinity, and the Media*. Newbury Park: Sage.
Crenshaw, K. 1991. "Mapping the Margins: Intersectionality, Identity Politics, and Violence against Women of Color." *Stanford Law Review* 43(6): 1241–1299.
Darder, A. 2015. *Freire and Education*. London: Routledge.
De Visser, N. 2006. *Objects in Conflict*. 1st ed. Amsterdam: Stitching Building Bridge.
Evans, N. 1980. *Education beyond School: Higher Education for a Changing Context*. London: Grant McIntyre.
Inoue, M., Nishikitani, M., & Tsurugano, S. 2016. *Female non-regular workers in Japan: their current status and health*. Japan: Ind Health.
Fanon, F. 1967. *Black Skin, White Masks* [Peau noire, masques blancs.], trans. C. L. Markmann. London: Pluto.
Freire, P. 1972. *Pedagogy of the Oppressed*. New York: Herder and Herder.
Freire, P. 1976. *Education, the Practice of Freedom*. London: Writers and Readers Publishing Cooperative.
Freire, P. 2014. *Pedagogy of Commitment: Paulo Freire*. London: Paradigm Publishers.
Freire, P., Freire, A. M. A. & de Oliveira, W. 2016[2014]. *Pedagogy of Solidarity*. New York: Routledge.
Freire, P. & Macedo, D.P. 1987. *Literacy: Reading the Word & the World*. London: Routledge.
Freire, P. & Shor, I. 1987. *A Pedagogy for Liberation: Dialogues on Transforming Education*. Basingstoke: Macmillan.
Friedman, A. 1999. On Feminism, Womanhood and Power among Israeli Women in Dafna Izraeli, Ariela Friedman, Henriette Dahan-Kalev, Hanna Herzog, Manar Hasan, Hannah Navve, & Sylvie Fogiel-Bijaoui (Eds.), Sex, gender, politics: Women in Israel. Tel-Aviv: Hakibutz Hameuh'ad. (In Hebrew)
Gates, H.L. 1986. *"Race," Writing, and Difference*. Chicago: University of Chicago Press.
Giroux, H.A. 1983. *Theory and Resistance in Education: A Pedagogy for the Opposition*. London: Heinemann Educational.
Giroux, H.A. 1988. *Schooling for Democracy: Critical Pedagogy in the Modern Age*. London: Routledge.
Goffman, E. 1956. *The Presentation of Self in Everyday Life*. Edinburgh: University of Edinburgh, Social Sciences Research Centre.
Grant, C., & Sleeter, C. 2007. *Doing Multicultural Education for Achievement and Equity*. New York: Routledge.
Herzog, H. 2009. "Feminist Perspectives on the Political." *Theory and Criticism* 34: 155–164. (In Hebrew.)
Hird, M. 1998. Theorising Student Identity as Fragmented: Some Implications for Feminist Critical Pedagogy. *British Journal of Sociology of Education*, 19(4): 517–527. Retrieved from http://www.jstor.org/stable/1393448
hooks, b. 2000a. *All about Love: New Visions*. London: Women's Press.

hooks, b. 2000b. *Feminism Is for Everybody: Passionate Politics.* Cambridge, MA: South End Press.
hooks, b. 2000c. *Where We Stand: Class Matters.* New York: Routledge.
Kaplan, M. & Miller, A.T. 2007. *Scholarship of Multicultural Teaching and Learning.* San Francisco, CA: Jossey-Bass.
Katz, Jackson. 1999. *Tough Guise: Violence, Media and the Crisis in Masculinity.* Video.
Kohl, Herbert, R. 1999. *I Won't Learn from You: And Other Thoughts on Creative Maladjustment.* Darby: Diane Publishing Company.
Luke, C. & Gore, J. 1992. *Feminisms and Critical Pedagogy.* New York: Routledge.
Mackie, R. 1980. *Literacy and Revolution: The Pedagogy of Paulo Freire.* London: Pluto Press.
McClure, L. 2000. "Feminist Pedagogy and the Classics." *The Classical World* 94 (1): 53–55. doi:10.2307/4352498
Minnich, E., O'Barr, J.F., &RosenfeldR.A. 1988. *Reconstructing the Academy: Women's Education and Women's Studies.* Chicago: University of Chicago Press.
Mohanty, C. 1988. "Under Western Eyes: Feminist Scholarship and Colonial Discourses." *Feminist Review* 30: 61–88. doi:10.2307/1395054
Newberry, M., Gallant, A., & Riley, P. 2013. *Emotion in Schools: Understanding How the Hidden Curriculum Influences Relationships, Leadership, Teaching, and Learning.* Bingley: Emerald.
Redfern, C. 2013. *Reclaiming the F Word: Feminism Today.* London: Zed Books.
Rich, A. 1973. *Diving into the Wreck: Poems 1971–1972.* London: W.W. Norton.
Saroyan, A. & Amundsen, C. 2004. *Rethinking Teaching in Higher Education: From a Course Design Workshop to a Faculty Development Framework.* Sterling, VA: Stylus Pub.
ShochatE. 2001. "Controversial Histories: from Eurocentrism to Polycentrism." In *Forbidden Reminiscences: A Collection of Essays.* Tel Aviv: Kedem. (In Hebrew.)
Slater, J.J., Fain, S.M., & Rossatto, C.A. 2002. *The Freirean Legacy: Educating for Social Justice.* New York: P. Lang.
White, S.K., White, J.M., & Korgen, K.O. 2014. *Sociologists in Action on Inequalities: Race, Class, Gender, and Sexuality.* Los Angeles: Sage.
Wolf, N. 1990. *The Beauty Myth.* London: Chatto & Windus.
Zalmanson-Levi, G. 2004. "Exclusion and Detachment of Youth—It Can be Done Differently." In *Inequality in Education*, ed. Golan Agnon. Tel Aviv: Babel. (In Hebrew.)
Zalmanson-Levi, G. 2012. *Basic Terms in Critical Pedagogy.* Retrieved from: http://www.criticalpedagogy.org.il/%D7%A1%D7%A4%D7%A8%D7%99% D7%AA%D7%94%D7%91%D7%99%D7%AA/%D7%9E%D7%90%D7%9E% D7%A8%D7%99%D7%9D/%D7%9E%D7%95%D7%A9%D7%92%D7%99% D7%9D%D7%9E%D7%A8%D7%9B%D7%96%D7%99%D7%99%D7%9D% D7%91%D7%A4%D7%93%D7%92%D7%95%D7%92%D7%99%D7%94% D7%91%D7%99%D7%A7%D7%95%D7%A8%D7%AA%D7%99%D7%AA/ta bid/136/Default.aspx (In Hebrew.)
Zinn, H. 1974. *Justice in Everyday Life: The Way It Really Works.* Cambridge, MA: South End Press. Retrieved from http://www.loc.gov/catdir/enhancem ents/fy1505/2002029156-d.html

3 Practical critical pedagogy
Developing educational materials on human rights and gender for children with students

The use of a creative process in small and diverse working groups, in this case the development of a children's book on human rights, represents a reconfiguration of the traditional classroom dynamic. These groups constitute spaces in which participants are able to work together and share ideas and experiences, establishing mutual recognition of the approaches and skills that other students bring to the class. This helps to foster a sense of equality on different levels: it establishes equality between all participants, recognizing it as a positive and necessary value; equality is thus practiced as an everyday phenomenon, and an awareness of language equality is promoted. The method also fosters a stronger sense of inter-group commitment. This chapter will use discourse and content analysis of data gathered via classroom observation during the working group sessions and also in interviews with the students one year after the course had ended to explore the processes behind the production of such material on the part of students of peace and human rights education and social change. I will focus on what language and character representations were used in this course; what was said but also what left unspoken, and how this was both the result and the cause of profound political and cultural dynamics that affected dialogs and relationships within the small working groups during the course. Ultimately, this chapter examines the political, cultural, and social meanings that are hidden within cultural and linguistic challenges, and the related dilemmas that surfaced during the courses. It analyses the ways in which feminist critical pedagogy practices of collaborative book writing enable students to deal with cultural and linguistic differences in order to create a more egalitarian linguistic space than that which exists in current world politics and society as a whole.

The discourse and content analysis placed its focus on aspects of identity such as representation and visibility in children's literature and videos, and the role of language. The course begins with an intersectional gender analysis inspired by the Bechdel test,[1] and focuses on questions of power and who most books represent. We critically explore racial, ethnic, and gender visibility (qualitative and quantitative representation) in children's books and discover that women and girls in children's movies and books tend to talk less than men and boys. Furthermore, we discover that black children are quantitatively fewer in children's books, and in conducting a qualitative evaluation we find that black children's social roles are either negative figures or subordinated characters, such as the black friend or the black doorman (Conley, 2011). We map the limited knowledge we have on marginalized groups and people and conserve the "danger of the single story" that turn into negative stereotypes that aren't always untrue, but they are harmful as they are uncomplete (Adichie, 2009).

Feminist critical analysis of content and discourse seeks to understand subjective perceptions through critical reflection, disassembly, and reconstruction. In the process of investigation, de-familiarization is established; that is to say, the analysis seeks to translocate the story and to see it in a new "extrinsic" light which illuminates fresh meanings that were hitherto concealed. This approach attempts to materialize the construction of social ideas as "truth" by investigating the processes of education and endeavoring to disassemble them. Peter McLaren and Joe Kincheloe maintain that the exposure and critical examination of power relations turns research into a transformative task linked to liberating people's consciousness (Kincheloe & McLaren, 2007). This is a step towards corrective social action and the promotion of human rights and equality within education.

The human rights education course program

The human rights education course is conducted as a semester course for MA students in "Social Change through the Arts" at the Academic College of Society and the Arts in Netanya, Israel, as well as an intense two-week long course at the University for Peace (henceforth UPEACE) in Costa Rica. The latter is an intense program which allows teachers, peace, gender, social workers, and NGO workers to condense their studies in one full day per week while they continue their ongoing work or studies. The course includes 12–15 lessons that focus on the critical analysis and mapping of children's books in regard to gender, ethnicity, race, and physical or mental abilities, followed by a creative process of book development that is inspired by personal and group narratives of the students based on human rights violations and examples of oppression that they may have experienced first-hand or as educators through their students (secondary trauma).

The course explores the notion of human rights, the educational work of human rights organizations and activists, and ways to advocate for human rights. It begins with an overview of the methodologies of human rights education, covering a wide range of civil and political, economic, social, and women's rights and their expression in educational (formal and informal) curricula and textbooks. The course underscores human rights education as a means of working towards achieving the universal ideals of justice and peace, aiming for a positive alternative to the deconstruction and critical reading of children's books and educational media in regard to human rights. The discussion of human rights violations in an open and safe environment facilitates empowering dialogue and learning whilst also giving the students and their experience of the world a voice (Freire & Shor, 1987). The multiplicity of students' experiences, narratives, and voices is heard in the way they express themselves in their spoken languages. Through the negotiation with other languages, other narratives, and other ideas students are exposed to a plurality of voices and perspectives (Freire, Freire, & de Oliveira, 2014).

More specifically, the course is designed to provide students with a practical tool to promote gender equality and equity, human rights education and explore the potential of human rights frameworks in an everyday context in and beyond schooling and school curriculums. The project aims to mobilize students to dream, develop, design, write, and produce an online video of a virtual children's book on human rights history and "herstory" about a human right of their choice.

The course is based on critical pedagogy theory with its primary objective to create an educational process which empowers its participants to become critical consumers of the knowledge and values that their societies promote and prioritize (Gor Ziv, 2013). Critical pedagogy theory and the tools derived from it strive to create a process that will help expose the complexity of reality as well as the current social and political status quo. This model explicitly locates the main cause of continued discrimination and conflict in cultural and human rights violations, social practices, and norms. A key emphasis is placed on the need for open and frank discussion regarding power structures which reinforce state institutions and underpin gender, social and cultural hierarchies. By highlighting seldom discussed topics and problems, critical pedagogy educators can help empower marginalized sub-groups within the classroom and thereby give them hope and an outlet for their political, communal, and personal concerns. The process can also uncover previously unacknowledged similarities between conflicting—and even "enemy"—sub-groups and begin to foster common actions and feelings of solidarity arising out of these similarities (Halabi & Reich, 2004).

The critical-pedagogy model emphasizes sensitivity to the cultural and socio-economic realities of the participants. Its aim is for teachers to work with students through educational tools like dialogue to create a positive alternative to their current state by uncovering hidden curricula and knowledge, and awakening a critical consciousness concerning their culture and experiences. Critical pedagogy also seeks to broaden students' understanding of the power structures inherent in society and of how such structures are reflected in the diverse groups of learners taking part in the workshop or the course (Gor Ziv, 2013).

Apart from critical pedagogy, the course also makes use of another educational model for gender equity, peace, and human rights education: The task-oriented method is built upon the belief that when conflicting groups are forced to jointly solve problems (or tasks) they, by necessity, develop cooperation mechanisms so that a pragmatic understanding between the participants can be reached. The logic behind this model of peace education is that dialogue encounters based upon common goals and objectives will lead to the creation of shared ideas and conclusions and joint solutions between the participants, thus forming a common bilateral ground for dialogue and cooperation. This ability to cooperate and coordinate is then extrapolated to other tasks and situations. If the groups can work together on one project, then these same cooperation mechanisms can be applied to peacebuilding and sustainable peace.

The task-oriented model of peace education grew out of criticism of the original intergroup-contact model, with the aim of improving upon it rather than wholly rejecting it. The most common critique of the contact theory is that it does not foster joint goals or objectives. In contrast, the task-oriented model aims to create an opportunity for dialogue between groups, where tools and skills for conflict transformation can be developed through problem-solving tasks based on real-life situations. The primary objective of this method is to develop dialogue out of a practical need for a peaceful and coordinated solution. Accomplishing tasks together as a unified group rather than as enemies or opponents results in greater understanding and tolerance. It is also hoped that, by sharing in the feeling of accomplishment, stereotypes, and hatred will be overcome.

During the course, students are asked to select a topic or human right that they would like to explore, and are required to debate and participate in a dialogue concerning that particular right. They must then reach some form of consensus within their working groups as to the kind of content and depiction that will be employed their plan to bring the project to fruition. This working process has the potential to generate a great deal of disagreement within the group as different needs and values may clash, yet these differences must be overcome if students are to successfully develop a united approach on matters such as illustrations, title selection, and the choice of rhyme and meter. The students share their views and needs, negotiating practical solutions in a manner similar to the critical dialog process, but develop their cooperative skills through the task-oriented method. The combination of the two models promotes both a practical positive outcome in a short period of time and facilitates a meaningful dialogue based on shared experiences.

The participants

The classes both at the Social Change and Arts College in Netanya, Israel, and at UPEACE consisted of 14–28 female-majority students from 21 to 60 years of age, most of them teachers or informal educators, as well as some social workers and NGO workers or volunteers from diverse working groups that may be referred to as "mixed groups." As noted by Enloe (2004), when we use the term "mixed groups" it is important to be clear about what this mix consists of, why we choose to refer to it as a mix, and how the people who are a part of this mix feel about the term. The participants at UPEACE consisted of peace educators (with both formal and informal education backgrounds), half of whom were scholarship holders of the Asian Peace Scholarship, and were from Cambodia, Thailand, Myanmar, Laos, Japan, and Vietnam. The other half of the students were from the USA, Mozambique, Turkey, Costa Rica, Mexico, Holland, India, and Canada. The university's diversity and multicultural environment were the main reasons for choosing UPEACE as a location for the study. The course is structured to allow dialogue around multicultural issues and to explore the use of local contexts and languages in peace and human rights work. Most students were participating in the course in order to work in a diverse group and to gain experience and knowledge from others.

The participants from the Social Change and Arts College were a small diverse group including Jewish-Israeli, Christian-Israeli, and Muslim Arab-Israeli women from Arab villages within Israel. As Jews and Arabs rarely meet in the Israeli public sphere in general and in higher education in particular, it is rare for them to have interactions and relationships on an equal footing. The small learning groups and even smaller working groups allowed them to experience, often for the first time, encounters where all participants were treated as equals. Although some participants elected to take the course because of the diverse groups of people involved, others were indifferent or even distrustful when faced with the prospect of working with other women from such a wide range of backgrounds. However, collaboration with the "other" was necessary in order to successfully complete the course. Some of the Arab students facing language difficulties in Hebrew had to rely on the Jewish students to proofread their work while hardly any of the Jewish students spoke any Arabic at all, meaning that, if they chose to submit the book/video in Arabic and Hebrew, they would need to completely rely on the Arab students for translation. The different ways in which the Jewish and Arab participants collaborated and clashed represented, in a nutshell, the minority–majority sociopolitical tensions that define society in Israel.

The dilemma of language: all languages are not equal

It is a common situation in post-colonial academic settings that the teaching and learning underway, while aiming to promote human rights, does so using the hegemonic language of the specific context and country. This section will examine the ambivalence in regard to the power and control that language represents, followed by a discussion of encounters concerning the languages that were used during the courses; in this case Arabic, English, and Hebrew.

Language is not merely a tool for communication but, importantly, it is inherently political. Language can be a representation and legitimization of culture, customs, and power. In any country that has experienced colonialism, immigration, or conflict, language is both a medium of dialog between different peoples and of the power dynamics of the groups involved. By educating in the hegemonic language, dominant groups gain control, power, and privileges; communication is not only easier for them, but the hegemonic group also determines what is right and how conversations will be conducted (Errington, 2008). This amounts, in effect, to a cultural commandeering of language. For the purpose of this book, the term "language" is meant to comprise both the spoken national language and the cultural language that reflects cultural capital and manifests itself in various skills and abilities, such as presenting in front of a classroom, working in academic settings, determining and controlling the discourse, and reflecting critically on a variety of topics. For native speakers, the language of tuition holds many advantages: English carries the highest cultural value; it allows students to read and write unimpeded and to express themselves in class without undue preparation; it also privileges with easier access to study materials, as well as access and control over the class discourse.

At UPEACE the hegemonic language and language of tuition is English, used as a native language only by a minority of students. Most students read and write English at diverse levels and sometimes struggle to express emotions and complex ideas. All reading materials, papers, and tests are conducted in English. In the course there is therefore a distinct and spoken power imbalance between native English speakers and those who are not. The privilege to express oneself in one's own native language is discussed and analyzed during the course. In Israel an equivalent situation arises when the groups in question are Palestinians or Israelis, new immigrants, or when participants belong to settled immigrant populations.

The participants of the course at the Social Change and Arts College in Netanya, Israel, reflect the Israeli population diversity and are thus linguistically and culturally diverse; Arabic and Hebrew are both official languages in Israel. In spite of this diversity, the main language used for communication among Israeli citizens, whether Jews or Arabs, is Hebrew. Most Arabs, who make up almost one quarter of the Israeli population, speak Hebrew with varying levels of fluency, while most Jews do not speak any Arabic at all. As such, then, the hegemonic language in Israel is Hebrew. The teaching language at the college is Hebrew and papers are to be written in Hebrew as well.

According to Karl R. White (1982) and Selcuk R. Sirin (2005), students from marginalized groups do not have equal chances in entering or succeeding in academic studies, and access to hegemonic upper-class language plays a major part in this exclusion. Students from groups with less cultural capital (i.e., with cultural characteristics conveyed through speech, attitudes, knowledge, and behaviors not highly valued by a specific social system) are less likely to finish their studies, complete tasks on time, and receive grades as high as those awarded to students from hegemonic groups, mainly due to language aspects (Bourdieu, Passeron, & Nice, 1990). By asking students to write and present in their national and cultural language instructors can forge a bond with students and engage them on an emotional and political level (Freire & Macedo, 1987). Moreover, as language expresses self-confidence, self-determination, culture, and values, it would seem fruitful to allow students to use their own language in a course on human rights education, a course requiring a particular level of political and personal involvement and dealing specifically with emotional and sometimes traumatic experiences (Zak & Halabi, 2006).

In Israeli schools and academia, the unequal, systematic, and discriminatory treatment of the Arab population (with curricula not being designed according to their cultural context, exams administered in literary rather than spoken Arabic, less funding and ministerial support, as well as the students' lack of access to cultural wealth and hegemonic knowledge) leads to the poorer performance of Arab schools (Maoz, 1998). The lack of access to university higher education in their own national language discriminates against the Arab population as compared to the Jewish population, with Arab women suffering the double burden of language as well as gender discrimination.

One requirement of the material produced in the class was that it must be submitted in at least two languages, with a view to widening the audience for the open-source material and enhancing the use of different languages. The opportunity to translate the collaboratively developed open-source children's book into their own languages encouraged students from linguistically marginalized groups to bring their culture and discourse to the fore. The participants were free to choose which languages were to be used and were prompted to reflect upon their choice. At the Social Change and Arts College, the projects needed to include at least Arabic, Hebrew, and/or English; at UPEACE, the choice was wider, and reflected the participants' backgrounds. This undermining of the linguistic hegemony came as a shock and strong political statement to the Jewish students and native English speakers, and as a pleasant surprise to the Arab students and non-native speakers in both institutions. An Arab student from the north described her astonishment and her intention to use her national and ethnic language. She also commented on her classmates' reaction:

> It was obvious from the get-go that this course would be conducted in Hebrew. It is also obvious that language conveys culture and personal identity. The fact that the instructor allowed us to write in any language we wanted was not received with much enthusiasm by the Jewish students. On the other hand, the Arab women were excited, although they wrote in literary rather than spoken Arabic; but in any case, they didn't deny the legitimacy of using Hebrew.

A conversation around the importance of language choices is not only necessary but also productive in the context of human rights discussions as well as in the process of developing a children's book on a particular human right. For instance, a book written in Spanish and English in the UPEACE context projects a strong statement about the equality between languages to the (predominantly US) English speaker, while a book written in Vietnamese and English is seen and discussed as a tool of communication to enlarge audiences and allow access to educational materials to people in Vietnam who do not speak English. In the Israeli context, Russian and Hebrew speak to the particular experience of interactions between immigrants from post-Soviet states and second- and third-generation Israelis. Stories written in English and Arabic and/or Hebrew exist in a Western global context and act as a bridge between the West and Middle Eastern communities. The use of Hebrew and Arabic together supports the legitimacy of both as equal-status languages, something which is of importance in the context of the Israeli–Palestinian conflict. The most commonly chosen combination in the Netanya course, English, Hebrew, and Arabic, helps to link the discourse within the classroom to wider global discussions on human rights and a more widely accessible humanist approach to education. In addition to Arabic and Hebrew, many of the class's participants also wanted their books to be in English, partly to make them more accessible for international audiences, but also because they saw English as a more prestigious language.

How power dynamics affect the use of languages is illustrated well by the case of two students who wished to write in Amharic and Tigrinya, two languages commonly spoken in Ethiopia. While these participants were fluent speakers of their chosen languages, they had not been brought up literate in them (although they were literate in Hebrew and English). Additionally, they were unable to find other members of their communities who could write in them. The impossibility of creating and publishing a simple children's book on human rights in their mother tongues prompted an important conversation on how languages are lost through immigration, mainly immigration from places considered less privileged and ranked below the new country. The new language then has a higher status in the community, the family and for individuals who speak it with their children and even their parents to enhance integration and gain a higher status (Alba, Logan, Lutz, & Stults, 2002). The students also discussed the role of parents in choosing which language(s) they wish their child to be conversant and literate in, reinforcing the notion that fluency in the hegemonic language is a requirement for upward social mobility and aspirations. Palestinian Israelis who send their children to Hebrew-speaking schools or parents in Latin America who send their children to English-speaking schools constitute further cases in point. This tendency can result in a situation where a child is fluent in a language (be it Arabic, Amharic, Spanish, or Tigrinya) but simultaneously illiterate in it.

I begin the first session of the class by asking the students which human rights were personally important to them, which, if any, of their human rights they felt had been violated when they were young, and what changes they would like to see in their society and community so that other children would not have to undergo the same experience. This initial process is a difficult one as many students at both institutions feel that the infringements they had experienced were too small to be noteworthy, or they felt they were too well-off or otherwise privileged for such things to happen to them (human rights violations being, in their view, things that happened elsewhere). For people from the northern hemisphere at UPEACE, human rights violations are things that happen in Africa; for African and Asian students they occur in remote areas; for Jewish-Israeli participants in Israel, human rights violations occur in remote places like Africa, whereas for Arab-Palestinians they are localized problems that happen to people in Gaza and the West Bank as a matter of routine.

As a class, we explored the concept of human rights by reading through the United Nations Universal Declaration of Human Rights together, discussing its origins and examining individual articles. We then came up with examples of each of these being fulfilled and violated. The students in both institutions were then asked to reflect on the articles of the Declaration and connect them to their own experiences on a personal, communal, and national level. At the beginning of the course many of the students arrived wishing to change things in their school, workplace, or country, motivated by experiences at the macro level. However, after exploring and studying examples of human rights infringements they began to relate to them on a much more personal level and produced educational materials that reflected the range of their own experiences. Their choice of topics included: better representation of children from different racial, religious and ethnic backgrounds; of children with physical disabilities; of child poverty; of experiences inspired by individuals they had met in their roles as teachers; raising awareness of the sexual abuse of children; the right to have a family, especially for those who do not fit within the cisgender heterosexual hegemony. Rather than deconstructing existing educational material, therefore, the students began their own creative process taking their own experiences as a starting point.

The example of Jihan, an Arab student, and Rachel, a Jewish student, is a case in point. Initially, Rachel did not wish to share her personal experiences, but after working with her class partner Jihan on their joint book she revealed that she had been brought up in a Kibbutz where every week a person who was responsible for the children would come around and empty out the contents of each child's drawer onto their bed. This person would then go through their belongings, throwing out anything he or she did not deem necessary or appropriate. Rachel recalled that none of the children had a space they could call their own, which no one else was allowed to touch. Through this reflection she saw the connection to the right to privacy and developed the idea of a children's book about a drawer that no one but the child who owned it was allowed to open. By writing this story, Rachel and Jihan produced a book that would not only help prevent similar things happening to other children; they also identified a legal framework to describe the feeling of violation she experienced as a child. She was able to create for herself and other children a narrative and a language to describe the kind of infringements that young people experience. Jihan linked the story to her experience as an Arab-Palestinian and was enthusiastic about promoting the right to privacy within her family and community.

The students were cautious in their selection of character names, deliberately choosing names that sound alike in Hebrew and Arabic (although they may not share the same meaning), thus underscoring the similarities of the two cultures rather than their differences. By so doing, they deliberately blurred identities to render it unclear whether a character was Jewish-Israeli, Muslim-Arab, or Christian-Arab. This prevented the creation of a hierarchy in the mind of the reader and emphasized the equality and right to respect held by all the children featured in the book.

Language as a human right was an important part of the group's discourse as well as concomitant feelings when we are unable to understand a language. The centrality of language and the importance of access to texts in one's own language were underscored by the political context in which the courses took place. As one course began in the spring of 2018, Israel recognized both Hebrew and Arabic as official languages. However, later that semester the Israeli government began work on a new nation-state bill which was finally passed into law in July 2018. The new law downgraded the status of Arabic from an official language to one which was accorded "special status." One consequence of this is that public signage no longer needs to be bilingual but would now be solely in Hebrew. This legal change had a profound effect upon the class. Thereafter, the creation of books that were in both Hebrew and Arabic became an extremely political statement and a symbol of how their designers would like their society to be. It is important to note here that within Israel and Arab regions there are no bilingual Arabic–Hebrew children's books. When books are produced bilingually it is almost always because they deal with the Israeli–Palestinian conflict. By exploring the concept of the validity and legitimacy of languages, therefore, the students were also by proxy examining cultural privileges in Israel, both within their communities and at a national level. Children's books are a way to explore such power dynamics in a safe manner, without having to directly deal with national and political conflicts.

For the students it was important to underscore not only the validity of multiple languages, but also their equality through visual means. In the case of the book *Om(a)er's Drawer*, Rachel and Jihan chose to address this issue by switching the order in which the languages appeared as the reader progressed through the book, each language alternately at the top and at the bottom, at the left and at the right of the page. This gesture served to normalize the appearance of them in a non-hierarchical structure, symbolizing that neither language should dominate the other. Additionally, in their illustration of the chest of drawers, in which each child had a drawer with his or her name written in both Arabic and Hebrew script, they chose to use Arabic spelling conventions for names even when they were written in Hebrew. For many Israeli Jewish children this would be the first time they had seen names like theirs written in Arabic orthography. While both languages are treated as equal in the book, the use of Arabic transliteration in the illustrations recognized the political context of the authors, in which Arabic is institutionally treated as lesser.

One instance at UPEACE concerned the creation of an open-source children's book about the right to seek asylum. One of the dilemmas the participants faced was whether to publish the book trilingually (in Arabic, Turkish, and Dutch), or to produce separate books in the respective languages. After much deliberation it was decided to publish the books separately and to produce them in different countries in order to foster higher access rates and to contextualize the book within the local culture. Another dilemma was how to critically and yet sensitively explain state policies around asylum-seeking and the rejection of refugee children's applications in a manner appropriate for children. The task that the group took on was to "translate" policy papers from different countries (including their own) into language comprehensible to children. In addition, the group, which consisted of three students from Turkey, Japan, and the Netherlands, wanted to have a critical framework concerning other human rights violations in a variety of countries, such as restrictions placed on women in Saudi Arabia, who were until recently prohibited from driving[2] and are required to wear specific clothing including the hijab, as well as the lack of social integration of black people in the Netherlands. The compromise agreed upon was that the other human right violations that were not directly related to refugee rights would be shown and presented artistically as illustrations. Thus, one of the book's protagonists, a girl who welcomes Ahmad, a refugee (Ahmad was chosen as one of the world's most common names), is uncovered and plays on the beach with toy cars and trucks. Later, the Dutch child who welcomes Ahmad but is affected by the anti-refugee broadcasting on television is black and comes across as non-gendered.

The employment of art as a language enabled the students to resolve the dilemma as to how to tell children about other human rights violations that are not connected to refugees but are nonetheless part of everyday life. It also opened a conversation about the importance of art as a language and how far one can take a conversation about racism and discrimination against children. On the one hand, children in these countries are the victims of human rights violations; on the other, the use of the book as educational material by parents and teachers may pose problems in structuring a dialogue around discrimination, especially when it comes to refugee rights. The overall feeling within the group was that it would be enough to present and process the key issue at hand. The illustrations, therefore, showed children playing, laughing, and talking, at times scared, but did not open up a verbal conversation around these related matters.

A group of Arab students chose to create a book and video about the inclusion of autistic children in educational media. Three out of the five were special education teachers and one had a family member who was autistic. They presented a draft of the book and video, which were in Arabic with English subtitles. They explained that in East Jerusalem, where they lived, a video in Hebrew would be impractical and potentially unusable for the teachers for whom the content would be intended. Moreover, they continued, its applicability in the wider Arab world would be greatly enhanced if it were in a language other than Hebrew. This proved provocative and the classroom dynamics became conflictual. Many of the Jewish students felt hurt and even betrayed by the group's choice not to use Hebrew in their video. That a group of Jewish-Israeli students found it uncomfortable to hear a presentation only in Arabic was a great source of conversation and debate:

"It is insulting and exclusionary that they [the Arab students] are presenting only in Arabic so that we [the Jewish students] do not understand," one student claimed angrily. "We do not understand you," other students repeatedly said during the presentation. "We will translate for you later," answered the Arab students. A few of the Jewish students felt that the Arabic-language presentation was intended to upset and patronize them and to make them feel left out as a revenge maneuver. "They are doing it on purpose, speaking Arabic over and over again next to us so we won't understand." Interestingly, Arab students' almost exclusive access to the Arabic language often has an intimidating effect on Jewish students. In a similar workshop in Germany, a native German-speaking student commented that it was "okay for them [the Arab students in the workshop] to write in Arabic if German is too difficult for now." Similar examples accrued also in a US group in regard to use of the Spanish language, the demand of the hegemonic group was that the book will be translated into Spanish and not written in it in order to maintain to original meaning of the English words.

Language as a means of communication, it seems, is easier for hegemonic groups in my courses to accept. However, when language is used as a form of political power, a sign of resistance, or a means to maintain one's culture during or post immigration, the reaction is often conflictual and the participants from the "host" or hegemonic culture feel intimidated.

Eva's choice of the word "now" in the above quotation represents the host's temporary patience, with the implicit expectation that one will "integrate" and learn to speak the hegemonic language as well. It is more difficult for German-language students to accept that German-Arab students (second-generation migrants) may wish to write in both German and Arabic. The use of Arabic by such individuals is seen to not even be an option, and is regarded as a sign of de-integration and resistance to the hegemonic norm.

This sparked a conversation about the power dynamics of majority–minority relations, with the group's Arabic speakers pointing out that no justification was needed for videos in the hegemonic languages (Hebrew and English; or only Hebrew). The group responsible for the book and video also argued that the lack of representation and the right to inclusion was an issue of particular relevance to Palestinian and Arabic-speaking schools, and that these materials presented a practical way of tackling the problem. The final video (in Arabic with English subtitles) was of an extremely high quality and generated the class's highest number of likes and shares online, largely from Arabic-speaking regions. However, Jewish students, uncomfortable with the production of a video partially or wholly incomprehensible to them, chose in response to create videos and books only in Hebrew – although ostensibly these materials promoted equity and equality. We talked about the language issue in class and the Arab students explained that it is harder for them to speak, write, and present in Hebrew. The Jewish students responded: "It is fine, then, as long as it is a means of communication and not a political statement against us." During the following year's course, the class discussed the issue earlier on and many groups made a concerted effort to create bilingual educational materials in both Hebrew and Arabic. The fact that the course product could be submitted in Arabic thus opened up numerous questions and fostered an enlightening dialogue, the feeling of inclusion, and also the opportunity to integrate one's own national and cultural identity into the course. "It is a unique experience," commented Maram, an Arab student. "I feel that I am fully myself in a course in which my language is heard."

Negotiating language issues of free speech

What can and what should be presented as material for human rights education? How far should one seek to expand the "other's" comfort zone in order to promote human rights? Are all rights equally important? What if someone is hurt by another's opinion? These are some of the questions that are raised when language and free speech are negotiated in workshops and classes.

The case of Noa's final project reflects the lesson of practical collaboration which is integral to the course. During the group discussion revolving around which human rights were of particular personal importance to the students, Noa shared her passion for the human right to family. Noa's son is gay and it was a source of pain and frustration for her that he was denied the right to an equal marriage and the opportunity to adopt children. She wanted to use her project to normalize queer and non-traditional family groups: for example, single parents, mixed families, and cases where grandparents are the primary caregivers. She also wanted to normalize the depiction of children engaged in activities that challenge traditional gender roles, such as boys helping with the housework at home. While designing her book, Noa, together with her two group members who were also Jewish, decided that they wanted to write it in three languages (Arabic, Hebrew, and English), thus making it more accessible and egalitarian, underscoring the book's message that all people and family types are equal. Noa's group spent a great deal of time brainstorming how to incorporate the family with two fathers in a way that did not emphasize this situation as unusual or special. Eventually they settled on introducing the family through the act of going out to get pizza, depicting the family activity without reference to the parents' sexual orientation.

The belief that gay parents should be treated as the equals of heteronormative couples might at first appear to be a mild statement in a human rights class. However, the topic did prove to be controversial for the more religious members of the class (who were Christian, Druze, Jewish, and Muslim). The discussion moved from LGBTQIA+ rights to questions of educational principles, asking when and what to tell children about sex and sexual orientation, questions about freedom of speech, as well as value conflicts as to not only what should be said, but also the where and how. An example would be the assertion that LGBTQIA+ rights is a private issue, one that should not be taken to the streets, and therefore should not be integrated into formal and informal educational curriculums.

Although group members who were uncomfortable with the depiction of a gay couple in a children's book did not change their minds, they nonetheless agreed to help Noa translate her story into Arabic. The compromise reached was that they did not take any active part in the development of the story, for instance writing or illustrating, and the translator asked that her work not be credited, partly from fear of the social backlash her involvement would receive. This compromise is a primary example of how, although cultural differences cannot always be erased, they can and sometimes must be transcended. Within the class's context (against the backdrop of the Israeli–Palestinian conflict), it was an important lesson that individuals with vastly different religious and secular beliefs can indeed work together and negotiate solutions.

During the discussion on Noa's project it was sometimes necessary for me as the lecturer to remind the participants of the human rights approach, stating that all people have a right to a family and that a consequence of free speech is also the right to represent issues which others might find uncomfortable or even hurtful. The solution that the group reached—to translate but not put their name to the work—recognized that while we may not always agree, we can still accept how others choose to live their lives. Thus the language discussion sparked by Noa's project in this case was not only an acknowledgment of the right held by others to express themselves but, conversely, the discovery that people have the right to *not* lay claim to a work, and that they can instead decide to disclaim ownership by distancing themselves from the creative process, product, and the implications of authorship.

Conclusion

Human rights are an issue that touches every aspect of society and people of every age and can be translated into concrete effects and practical outcomes if children are introduced to the topic in relevant ways that engage and empower them. The aim of the course Human Rights Education through Open Source Children's Books is to provide a space in which educational materials with a focus on human rights can be created. Students are asked to recognize and question mechanisms of knowledge production and power structures. During the course it becomes evident that language issues are of primary importance, as they reflect and embody the essence of social tensions and conflicts. Students become increasingly aware of the fact that explicit and inherent power is manifested in language and visual cues, and that they can use those mechanisms themselves to promote discourse on rights and inclusion.

In contrast to the deconstruction process students encounter in seminars, where they analyze and criticize until they are left with an array of deconstructed components, it is my aim for this course to provide students with a positive alternative, by giving them a tool to effect meaningful and hopeful social change. I want them to (re)claim their voices by translating their experiences into stories that are then shared openly and freely. This is why the books produced in the class place their emphasis not on the violation but on the protection and celebration of human rights, and aim to lend a sense of fulfilment and even fun to this serious issue.

When designing this course, I endeavored to respond to the need of teachers and children concerning the lack of practical, hands-on educational media and curricula in respect to human rights, and thereby create a ripple effect by changing the reality of the students who will in turn change the realities of their own students. My observation has been that questioning narratives and our use of language(s) turns out to be an optimal starting point.

Notes

1 The Bechdel test asks three questions on a given film: 1. Are there more than two women in a film and do they have names? 2. Do the women talk to each other? 3. Do they talk about any topic that is not relating to a man? *Bechdel Test Movie List*, April 10, 2014. http://bechdeltest.com/.
2 Something to the effect that the ban on driving for women was gradually lifted in 2017–2018, but remains a conflicted and highly politically charged issue, with the detention and imprisonment of the movement's figureheads.

References

Adichie, C. 2009. Transcript of "The danger of a single story". [online] Ted.com. Available at: https://www.ted.com/talks/chimamanda_adichie_the_danger_of_a_single_story/transcript?language=en [Accessed March 22, 2019].
Alba, R., Logan, J., Lutz, A., & Stults, B. 2002. Only English by the Third Generation? Loss and Preservation of the Mother Tongue among the Grandchildren of Contemporary Immigrants. *Demography*, 39(3): 467–484. Retrieved from http://www.jstor.org/stable/3088327
Bourdieu, P., & Passeron, J.-C. 1990. *Theory, Culture and society. Reproduction in Education, Society and Culture* (2nd ed.) (R. Nice, Trans.). Thousand Oaks, CA, US: Sage Publications, Inc.
Conley, E. 2011. "Representation of Race in Children's Picture Books and How Students Respond to Them." Education Masters. Paper 47.
Enloe, C.H. 2004. *The Curious Feminist: Searching for Women in a New Age of Empire*. Berkeley, CA: University of California Press.

Errington, J. 2008. *Linguistics in a Colonial World: A Story of Language, Meaning, and Power.* Oxford: Blackwell. http://www.loc.gov/catdir/toc/ecip0715/2007014517.html

Freire, P., Freire, A.M.A., & de Oliveira, W.F. 2014. *Pedagogy of Solidarity.* Walnut Creek, CA: Left Coast Press.

Freire, P. & Macedo, D.P. 1987. *Literacy: Reading the Word & the World.* London: Routledge.

Freire, P. & Shor, I. 1987. *A Pedagogy for Liberation: Dialogues on Transforming Education.* Basingstoke: Macmillan.

Gor Ziv, H. 2013. *Feminist Critical Pedagogy and Education for a Culture of Peace.* Tel Aviv: Mofet Institute.

Halabi, R. & Reich, D. 2004. *Israeli and Palestinian Identities in Dialogue: The School for Peace Approach.* New Brunswick, NJ: Rutgers University Press.

Kincheloe, J. & McLaren, P. (eds) 2007. *Critical Pedagogy: Where Are We Now?* New York: Peter Lang.

Maoz, M. 1998. *Middle Eastern Politics and Ideas: A History from Within.* London: I.B. Tauris.

Sirin, S.R. 2005. "Socioeconomic Status and Academic Achievement: A Meta-analytic Review of Research." *Review of Educational Research* 75: 417–453.

WhiteK.R. 1982. "The Relation between Socioeconomic Status and Academic Achievement." *Psychological Bulletin* 91: 461–481.

Zak, M. & Halabi, R. 2006. *When the Present Are Absent.* Neve Shalom: Neve Shalom Institute for Peace.

4 Creating images
Discovering hidden gender stereotypes about the self and the Other

This chapter is based on research that analyzed unequal gender relations and gender inequality among Palestinian and Jewish participants who defined themselves as men and women[1] of dialogue encounters organized in Israel. Major themes of gender analysis informed and enriched a creative grassroots dialogue process involving some 400 participants (of whom 22 were interviewed for this research), as well as 22 facilitators. National-ethnic and gender-based stereotypes were illustrated through drawing, ice-cream sculpting, and in-depth conversations which were facilitated in a manner conducive to new insights and learning. Follow-up research was conducted in an international setting at the University for Peace in Costa Rica (henceforth UPEACE). Here, MA students of peace studies, gender studies, media and peace education and human rights studies were asked to divide into (separate) gender-isolated groups of five to seven participants and draw a man and a woman. This chapter will describe the method and explore how it helps participants to critically analyze their own reactions to stereotypes they hold in respect to the Other and themselves. In addition, I will show how the method fosters open dialogue about power dynamics, social constructions and racial, ethnic, and sexual and gender hierarchies.

The method presented here can be instrumental in dealing with sensitive topics in peace work, development, and human rights education. The drawing of one's own and other genders (binary and fluid according to the groups' choice) is inspired by thoughts about language and "automatic stereotyping"[2] both of the self and of the Other, in terms of gender-related social, professional, and family roles (e.g., she, he) or neutral perceptions (it, I, the) and how identities are constructed based on complex stereotypes. Experiments among students and professionals demonstrate that gender information imparted through language automatically influences people's judgments, but also that stereotypes can be broken as a result of dialogue and educational conversations (Banaji & Hardin, 1996).

In order to foster reflection on and analysis of stereotypes about the self and the Other, and to provoke a conversation around gender-based stereotypes and identity construction, the internalization of social roles, beauty myths, and beauty standards, the practice of drawing images under time pressure is a useful tool to lay open deeply ingrained stereotypes that participants may not wish to acknowledge, even to themselves. The practice is based on the theoretical assumption that stereotypes can and should be broken, and that stereotypes cause harm by fostering discrimination and objectification. Furthermore, there is an assumption that prejudices based on gender may be causally linked to higher rates of sexual harassment, stress, and low self-esteem due to perceived dissonance between the notion of the ideal or acceptable self and one's own self-image (Major, Quinton, & Schmader, 2003).

The method presented in this chapter provides a tool to counter insufficient discourse about self-stereotyping and the ways in which stereotypes are constructed (Solórzano & Yosso, 2002). It challenges traditional social science, which "tells stories" behind the facade of a given hegemonic truth and "objective" research. As Shulamit Reinharz and Lynn Davidman point out, research processes inform power structures and must necessarily be questioned (Reinharz & Davidman, 1992). When critical race methodology intersects with gender analysis and feminist critical pedagogy it offers a space to map and conduct research grounded in the experiences and knowledge of marginalized groups (Enns & Forrest, 2005). This may initiate a dialogue among group members but also catalyze participants to reflect on their own internalized stereotypes. The practice of drawing (out) stereotypes is a theoretical, methodological, and pedagogical tool to challenge racism, sexism, and classism by raising awareness of and fostering dialogue on our own profoundly hidden and internalized identity constructions.

Gender-based stereotypes

Gender-based stereotypes are crude generalizations as to the gender attributes, differences, and roles of persons and groups. Gender stereotypes can be positive or negative, but they rarely convey accurate information about a person or group of people. When society or a group a priori applies gender assumptions regardless of factual confirmation, they are perpetuating gender stereotyping. Sex and gender stereotypes are the assumptions that a person of a particular gender is acting or will act in a particular way due to their gender and that he or she thus has a specific social role. Up until the 1990s, several studies claimed that boys had a preference for male-connoted toys and games, while girls had a liking for what were considered feminine toys and games. However, the research in question was based on procedures and methods that relied profoundly on gender-based stereotypes about toys, objects, and activities and was thus heavily biased (Ruble & Martin, 1998). The performance of masculinity and femininity is rooted in very early formative experience and internalized at a young age by the behavior of people around us; by toys, clothes, children's books, commercials, movies, computer games, and, last but not least, both formal and informal education. Gender performance is akin to an automatic program, a part of our identity that can frequently be activated by various triggers so that we act according to gender stereotypes even against our better knowledge. Recently, gender-based research was expanded to take into account the effect of the aforementioned objects when studying the development of gender constructs and self-stereotypes (Campbell, 2002).

Traditionally, gender-based stereotype research has focused on children's descriptions of female and male attributes in studies (e.g., Williams, 1975) that mapped and explored children's knowledge of gender stereotypes. Young children were asked to state which of given characteristics were female and which were male. The research proved that even children as young as two years old associated dominant traits and strength with masculinity, and gentleness, beauty, and submissiveness with femininity. It is a case in point that demonstrates that people's consciousness from a very early age is shaped by the social construct of gender: they are thus "ingendered" into social roles and perform accordingly (Butler, 1993; Stiehm, 1994).

The mechanism of stereotyping

Observing and analyzing stereotypes and prejudices from different angles sheds light on the mechanism of stereotyping. It has been shown that the presence of stereotypes in an environment establishes and furthers people's bias of others in the direction of the stereotype. The research of Chiu, Hong, Lang, Fu, Tong, and Lee (1998) demonstrates analogous activation effects on self-stereotyping. The results of their study, which exposed young people and high-school students to stereotypical materials, showed an increase in both stereotyping and self-stereotyping tendencies. At the same time, their study revealed that it was possible to reduce stereotyping and self-stereotyping by presenting other examples.

The Other (or Otherness) are important concepts in contemporary sociology, gender studies, peace studies, development, and philosophy. It is the counterpart of the modernist terms of Same or Sameness, related to the idea that there is a blessed state of equality if everything is the same, and describing a person or phenomenon in terms of similarity to the notion of the "I" (Friedman, 2013). This idea is related to the concept of "color-blindness" that actively ignores identity politics and race-based experiences (hooks, 1990). It is often linked to a perspective that can only be adopted by members of hegemonic groups. In the case of the intersectionality of racial and sexual stereotypes we will look at gender, ethnicity, and race blindness as part of a privileged discourse, reflecting on stereotypes of the self and Other (Brown-Jeffy & Cooper, 2011).

One definition of the Other is the way one perceives others in relation to the self. Emmanuel Levinas considers the Other as "otherwise than being," in other words, different from the self (the being) and as a non-place where, on the one hand, the one is selfless and in direct contact with the Other, and, on the other hand, in reflection, a place where the self can differentiate itself from the Other on a thematic level (Levinas, 1974). Otherness, according to Levinas, is reflected in the saying "to be in the other person's shoes," in its extreme meaning of not being oneself. While the experience of Otherness is stressful, painful, and cannot be duplicated as an intentional act, it is where ethics—the ethics of non-indifference—emerge. Furthermore, it is in and through the moment of interaction that the one and the other gain, retroactively, their meaning.

"Being in the other person's shoes" is precisely the moment where one is stripped of one's stereotypes and prejudices but ironically feels disempowered. When one "returns" to the self, one needs to re-establish oneself and talk about the experience of being the Other and not oneself. And there stereotyping begins. According to Levinas, language itself—the way in which we explain reality to ourselves—is a stereotyping mechanism in which words and ways of expressing ourselves linguistically are only traces to the Other. Not a full representation, but rather the Adichie's single story, condensed to a stereotype, we tell ourselves about the Other (Adichie, 2009).

Simone de Beauvoir in *The Second Sex* termed the Other "a minority." She argues that "minority" is a political and psychological state of mind rather than an absolute number of people. She explains that women are the Other for men; the man is the subject while women are his complementary objects. A woman is defined and differentiated in reference to man and not in reference to herself: "She is the incidental, the inessential as opposed to the essential, while he is the Subject, he is the Absolute—she is the 'Other'" (de Beauvoir, 1949).

De Beauvoir further linked the Otherness of women to stereotypes and prejudices concerning the racial and ethnic Other. She describes travelers who share a train compartment and argues that the smallest differences can lead to the construction of the fellow traveler as an Other with negative connotations which might even lead to rudeness or vulgarity. She herself, for instance, is always aware of being a woman whereas the men around her have the privilege to forgo such categories and think of themselves as "people" rather than "men" (a case of "gender blindness" that connects to the concept of race blindness). In small towns, de Beauvoir continues to explain, the townspeople look upon those who are from foreign places as "strangers," with suspicion and even with fear. Immigrants, refugees, and migrant workers are "foreigners" and seen as Other in many countries (de Beauvoir, 1949). Minorities and women are the ultimate Other, as the concoction of Otherness in contrast to the self is based on a political "unity and sameness" ideology of race or ethnicity. If we are to look at gender inequities in employment and connect them with gender-based stereotypes we can see that all available statistics indicate that men earn significantly more than women. This remains true no matter what year the figures are from, or whether they are weighted according to age, labor force status, or educational achievement. The reasoning is often due to social and family social constrictions in regard to the division of labor but is also connected to the worth men have over women in the labor market and in society in general (Gunderson, 1989). One may argue that earning less for the same job, based on gender and race, may lead to self-stereotyping and preconceptions of the quality of one's work. Further, promotions are often given to Others in the workplace who look, behave, and talk like the person doing the promoting; women are thus frequently passed over for a position by dominant bosses (even female bosses) because they are not "like us." This "us" is the ultimate subjective while women (and other marginalized groups) are the Other—de Beauvoir's "second sex." Gender studies, an academic field that overlaps with post- and neo-colonial studies, has developed gender analysis tools that have also proved adaptable to the analysis of social arrangements between ethnic identities and national identities. Gender analysis is an approach that focuses on a gender-oriented perspective as the fundamental basis of researching the power dynamics between different genders and the intersectional crossover with other identities. Feminist research based on gender-segregated data (how the same situation affects the genders differently) may also aim to bring about social change by advancing progressive gender-sensitive practices instead of merely explaining, defining, or clarifying the world around us. Feminist research contrasts with traditional and conservative research on issues related to gender (Neander & Scott, 2006).

The ability and willingness to explore stereotypes in the presence of what is considered an Other is difficult and requires social and individual courage and encouragement, particularly in conflict situations (Halabi & Zak, 2006) as was the case for my research. Female and male students of gender and human rights classes were asked to draw men and women in different contexts. The practice of drawing in the safe space of a workshop allows students to challenge heteronormative and hegemonic beauty standards and the ways in which social gender constructions are accepted and preserved.

The method

In sessions that deal with gender conflicts and gender stereotypes the practice of separating participants into gender-isolated groups are used as described above; such groups (which may include a non-binary group) discuss issues relating to their own gender in a "safe" environment. The findings of each group are then presented to the other groups at a later stage. Part of the dialogue conducted is the presentation of needs; for example, female groups often request of male groups that women be taken seriously and appreciated and be not objectified or touched without consent, whereas male groups ask for women to comfort them and support them more, to provide emotional encouragement, and to help them with their personal development. As a part of this practice, participants are given a large sheet of paper or alternatively (to increase time pressure) a block of ice cream. They are then invited to draw or sculpt an image of their collective or individual self and of the Other(s) gender (s); they are also told that the whole group will analyze and reflect on the outcome. Most groups choose to create images of the male and the female genders, although all groups are invited to create images of any gender that they feel represents them or is different from them according to their collective or individual views. For women this process often seems easy and natural, presumably because they are used to working with other women, and teamwork and collaboration appears even easier for non-binary groups. For men, who are often used to relying on women during artistic projects and for emotional reflection, the process of separating themselves from the women brings complications in my experience. Some men in my seminars have asked to join the women's groups just as observers. When the women refused, they felt rejected and angry, which was then often reflected in their drawings.

A risk of the exercise is that it may reinforce a monolithic, binary image of gender and strengthen participants' stereotypes of what women and men are and what a nationality is. The critical theory behind the research is that there are no such things as fixed images of "a woman" or "a man," but rather a fluid and changing variety of masculinities and femininities that differ according to context and circumstances, and across cultures.

The exercise described here, carried out in an Israeli–Palestinian setting, was designed as a new way to render visible stereotypes in Jewish–Palestinian encounters. Participants gathered in uniform Jewish and Palestinian groups (meaning the national and ethnic identities used in Israel for Jewish-Israelis and Palestinian-Israelis, the latter including Muslims, Christians, and Druzes). The groups were asked to paint or draw a Palestinian and a Jew. Using innovative and creative tools in relatively traditional workshop settings, the participants often divulged not only their stereotypes of the other group but, perhaps even more importantly, their self-stereotypes as well. Evaluative interviews suggested that many participants had learned to identify their own stereotypes.

The rarity of opportunities to encounter the Other on an equal footing may reinforce negative stereotypes in both the Jewish and the Palestinian communities in Israel and leads to a lack of knowledge of the other ethnic and national group. Jewish and Palestinian children and young adults rarely meet and have almost no opportunity to encounter each other's opinions and ideas. They have only few opportunities for personal and social interaction. They hold negative views of each other and often also of themselves in relation to the other group. In peace work and the facilitation of dialogue encounters the intersectional common stereotypes are mixed with gender stereotypes. Thus, you might have a discourse in a group in Israel in which the following stereotypes play a role: Arab-Palestinian women are shy, Jewish-Israeli men are assertive and aggressive while Arab-Palestinian men are easily seduced by Israeli women. What is important to remember is that the stereotypes that are at the back of the facilitators' minds are often reflected in the instructions, language, and mirroring of the group.

Ten sessions of dialogue encounters were observed between 2004 and 2010 in Neve Shalom, Nir School, and Givat Haviva, involving 400 male and female participants, half of whom were Palestinian-Israeli and half of whom were Jewish-Israeli, between 16 and 28 years of age. Twenty-two participants and twenty-two facilitators were interviewed before, during and after the encounters about their experiences and reflections, using an open interview format. The interviews (involving narrative storytelling) were inspired by gender-based/feminist research methodologies and intersectional analysis, with participatory and

Creating images 75

inclusive methods, research based on participants' viewpoints, and taking into account the values and experiences of women and marginalized groups. Almost all Israeli-Palestinian dialogue groups were led by two facilitators, one Jewish and one Palestinian. Most often, these were a Jewish woman and a Palestinian man, all Israeli citizens. The facilitator of the dominant group was usually a member of the power-deprived gender and the facilitator of the power-deprived group was usually a member of the dominant gender, the facilitator of the marginalized group was a member or the dominant gender. This was done intentionally, as a way to balance historically unequal power relations. The focus, however, usually stayed on the national-identity divide and ignored the gender divide. Thus, the complex asymmetry between the facilitators remained largely undiscerned and implicit.

Jewish facilitators were usually perceived (and perceived themselves) as members of the oppressing dominant group, although they were apologetic and dissenting. Palestinian facilitators were usually perceived (and perceived themselves) as members of the oppressed group on the national level (Halabi & Zak, 2006). One of the research hypotheses questioned why there was so little awareness of the oppression that female facilitators experienced as women in the dialogue process. For instance, control and power were often exercised by male Palestinian facilitators towards their co-facilitators, who were female Jews. The latter, in turn, tended to sense their roles as penitent oppressors and meanwhile disregarded how their political perception was in fact feeding into the control mechanisms under which they were subjected as women. These gender dynamics remained largely unnoticed, as the gender divide is rarely acknowledged. Our research therefore concentrated on two aspects: the underestimation and sometime invisibility of gendered power relations as a dynamic affecting the different groups and their participants, and the measurable disregard of female participants' and facilitators' feminine language within the groups, which was in keeping with commonlyheld gender-based stereotypes.

The following story introduces the predominance of ethnic/national identity (Jewish or Palestinian) over the gender-identity discourse in participants' recounting of these dialogue processes. It may reveal some of its implications. Muna (34), a female Palestinian facilitator, explained:

> I would like to start with a story that best demonstrates for me the gender inequality and gender oppression in dialogue encounters: we held a session at the Nir School about gender, the group talked about the division of labor in the household and why men do not

"help" women in the house, and whether the term "help" is appropriate and whose work it is anyway.

We divided the groups into mixed sub-groups [Palestinians and Jews] so that they could go and do the work outside. We had a Palestinian boy, 16 years old, in the group who said in the middle of discussion things like "What?" and "Ha?" [making facial expressions and noises of disrespect – G.H.] and could not sit still and jumped around.

This boy asked me—when they could go outside to work—whether he could go to his room to rest. I said "no." He asked in Arabic, "Please, I just want to go and rest." I said it's a learning space and time now and that he has to keep on working with his group and sleep later. Then he asked my Jewish male co-facilitator: "You are the man, what do you say?" and my co-facilitator said that if he has to, then he can go to his room.[3]

The person asking—a boy—perceives the facilitator, a woman of his own ethnic origin, as the Other. Still, typically the gender component of the participant's and facilitator's identities in such cases tends to go unnoticed and is hardly ever talked about, either during the dialogue encounters or during the facilitators' meetings, although it is very strongly present.

[…]

I got very upset. We just finished a conversation in the co-facilitators team about how to integrate gender into the general dialogue curriculum and came up with strategies to do so, and still he is "being a man" and letting this boy go while making me look like the bad, evil female facilitator, although the boy is from "my own" group.[4]

The facilitators (and through them the participants) often preserve the concept of "their group," meaning a sub-group of all Jewish-Israelis for the Jewish facilitator, and a sub-group of all Palestinian-Israelis for the Palestinian facilitator. For example, if there is something difficult to bring to the attention of one sub-group, then the facilitator from the same national/ethnic identity is expected to do that by reflecting and mirroring. In groups that have been working well for a substantial period of time, the facilitator from one national/ethnic identity can reflect and mirror the other national/ethnic identity group. Muna in this case felt it to be her responsibility and interest to keep the Palestinian male participant from "her" national group in the dialogue while the boy was leaning toward seeing the male facilitator as "his" point of reference, notwithstanding his national/ethnic identity. This confusion in respect to gender and national loyalties appears at various levels of the group dynamic. Frequently, both Palestinians and Jews valued the words and statements of the Jewish facilitator more than those of the Palestinian facilitator (Sonnenschein, Halabi, & Friedman 1998). However, after the national/ethnic/racial stereotypes have been broken, whenever the gender component enters the equation it seems to override the national/ethnic/racial component.

Male solidarity (as well as female solidarity) often creates a stronger (gender-based) identity than solidarity based on one's national identity, and this "gendered solidarity" can significantly impact upon the dialogue process. The facilitators, on the other hand, expect and promote national and ethnic solidarity rather than solidarity based on gender identity. Muna would like to be the Palestinian group facilitator and she feels that she is becoming the "girls' facilitator," which leaves her mainly with the Palestinian female participants, presumably because the Jewish male facilitator is seen by the Jewish female participants as representing their stronger identity.

National identity stereotypes override gender stereotypes

When national-identity stereotypes break down, therefore, they may be transformed into gender stereotypes which, in a way, serve as a common ground for both Jews and Palestinians.

Pnina (35), a female Jewish facilitator, testifies:

> The same colonialist stereotypes the Jewish group held of Palestinians were transformed into gender-based stereotypes of women, mainly Palestinian women. Instead of the image of a Palestinian who likes to work hard, serve, and satisfy needs and wants, the stereotypes were transformed into either the image of "motherly" women in general or into the image of women as sexual objects. The stereotypes were a bit different for Palestinian and Jewish women, but the mechanisms behind them were the same. For example, they drew the Palestinian women as cooking, cleaning, taking care of everybody and the Jewish women as serving food in sexy clothes, hinting at sexual services. Maybe this is what they wanted. No. This *is* what they wanted.

I have observed earlier that, when depicting a Jew, the Palestinian participants sometimes chose to depict her as a female (in 20 percent of the cases) and in a manner meant to ridicule. As for the Jewish group, 50 percent of the participants chose to depict the image of a Palestinian as male and the other half as female. When an image of a suicide bomber was drawn by the groups, it was female in two cases and male in one.

Discussion of results

Self-stereotyping

Self-stereotyping is more common within subordinate or marginalized groups but can also be found in dominant privileged groups. Women tend to carry more negative stereotypes about themselves and to objectify their selves and their bodies based on societal expectations (Frederickson & Roberts, 1997). Thus, women are given to self-objectification and eating disorders (Greenleaf, 2005) and sometime engage in body shaming of themselves and others, both of women and men.

Women, men, and children have completely different views of their bodies and women tend to be dissatisfied with their bodies and to translate their body (dis)satisfaction into feeling undesirable, unappreciated, and even unloved. The stereotypes that women have about their own bodies and their identity lead to a destructive body image (Grogan 1999) and have a destructive effect on their bodies (due to diets, "sausaging,"[5] mutilation, and surgery). When women draw Palestinians and Israelis and also men and women, the images of women often represent the "ideal woman" according to what Goffman calls the internalization of the infantilized and unstable image performed for the "male gaze": a thin, young, fully and perfectly made-up, long-haired woman (Goffman 1956). When men draw images of men, whether of a Palestinian and an Israeli or of a man in a gender workshop, they draw hyper-masculine men, well-muscled, often with the symbols of economic, social, and political power (e.g., uniforms and suits which nevertheless show the muscular bodies underneath). Palestinian men might also be represented as powerful landowners, shown by the symbol of an olive tree.

When asked to draw their own national image, Palestinians often selected a religious rural person, even if they themselves were non-religious urban dwellers. In all ten sessions, the image chosen to represent a typical Palestinian was male and either very religious or very traditional. The groups also chose to imbue the Palestinian image with a nationalistic character, such as waving a Palestinian flag or other Palestinian symbols of national pride. In half of the cases, they used the symbol to integrate the image of Handala—a cartoon by the Palestinian political cartoonist Naji al-Ali of a Palestinian refugee boy with his hands clasped behind his back. The choice by mixed gender groups of a male persona for the image of a Palestinian echoes the gender role of masculine protection. In addition, the depiction of a male character can be interpreted as the group's preferred representation intended for broader society, since politicians and leaders of the community are most often men.

Palestinian participants also chose a male to depict a typical Israeli Jew in eight out of the ten sessions: a male soldier carrying a weapon. In half of the cases he was covered with blood to suggest recent killings. In the two cases in which the Palestinian group chose to draw a woman to depict a typical Israeli, the image showed a highly attractive (sexy) and almost naked soldier. She also carried a weapon, was wearing a very short skirt, and smoking a cigarette, which can be interpreted as symbolizing promiscuity. In both cases this image of the Jewish female had blonde hair.

Jewish-Israeli participants most often chose a strong male to represent Jews. In half of the 40 cases of this sample the man wore a traditional kibbutz hat from the 1940s and 1950s, and carried agricultural tools. In 40 percent of the cases the male image was in possession of high-tech tools such as a computer. In 30 percent of cases the male image was drawn as protecting his family. The family—girlfriend/wife, parents, and siblings—were shown at home and in the background. When the home was drawn it was a classic, European-style home with red roof tiles and a small garden.

Jones (1997) argues that it is a common practice for subordinate groups in society to present themselves as more progressive than they feel they actually are: that they are trying to hide the stereotypes they hold of themselves and portray themselves as more "modern" in accordance with what they perceive as modern. When drawing the image of a Palestinian, in 70 percent of cases the Jewish-Israeli participants drew a low-class laborer doing hard menial work, such as cleaning a shopping mall, serving food, or washing a car, and wearing Western baggy and dirty clothes. The image of the Palestinian as a poor, dirty person is deeply rooted in the Israeli Jewish youth discourse (as it is in other majority hegemonic groups in conflict zones). Interestingly, all the groups drew their own image as a male. This was true both for the Palestinian and the Jewish groups. Even when the majority of the group's members were female, their collective "self" was represented by a male.

Analyses of stereotypes raised in an innovative, creative dialogue process

Four different stereotypes feature in the interviews for this study, all of which are indicative of power relations. Our hypothesis is that other dialogue processes dealing with similar power structures will face somewhat similar gender-related power dynamics and gender-based stereotypes.

The first is the stereotype of the promiscuous Jewish woman: According to this, Jewish women are easy to seduce, and their participation in the dialogue encounters is with the primary goal of meeting someone with whom to have sex. Their liberal modern clothing is interpreted as a symbol and proof of their promiscuity.

The second stereotype is that Palestinian men are only interested in having sex with white Jewish women. This stereotype is well known to be applied to men from non-white, minority groups and, as shown already, is adopted by them, as well. The stereotype rests primarily on the assumption that having sex with and/or the sexual and amicable attention of white women will make men from minority groups feel more socially accepted and respected by the white majority. This is an intersectional stereotype (national/ethnic and gender), reinforced by the prejudice in Israeli society that Palestinian men would like to sexually take advantage of Jewish women, either by raping them or by seduction, and that they would attack them physically if and whenever they are able to do so.

The third stereotype is that of the shy, innocent, and naive Palestinian woman who knows little about relationships between the sexes and is shocked and embarrassed when the issue of sexual or romantic relationships is raised.

The fourth stereotype that—according to the interviews—was reinforced during the dialogue process is that Jewish men will sell "their women" (another stereotype) in order to create a male bond with other males, in this case the Palestinian male participants.

By disregarding the issue of gender in the groups, the facilitators were communicating that the stereotypes encountered in the groups were connected with national/ethnic identity and related challenges only. Anything that happened beyond the range of this lens, even if stereotypical and harmful to subgroups or individual participants who are part of the process, remained invisible. By ignoring the gender issue, the facilitators were further legitimizing and encouraging sexist behavior. The stereotype of the Jewish women's promiscuity, for instance, is reinforced by the fact that it is blatantly not addressed, and even treated as irrelevant, when raised by both facilitators and participants, in spite of the explicit aim of these encounters to address stereotypes and prejudices. The message sent to the groups by the facilitators when making gender stereotypes invisible is that sexism and prejudices based on gender are neither important nor harmful. Thus, in the dialogue and dialogue encounters the focus remained on the tolerance discourse rather than on the subordination of women in society. Mia, a 29-year-old female Jewish facilitator, explains:

We were talking in the group about the post-colonialist term "historical amnesia" and I wanted to yell, "Hey, women were forgotten in history—hello ..." It is so relevant to talk about gender. I think I even said something, but it didn't fly in the group—they talked about it a bit and then it was neglected, hey, you know what, forgotten—like women.

The facilitators' act of ignoring gender tensions and gender-based stereotypes when they were raised may have several different reasons. One identified in this study alludes to the sensitive connection between gender and national identity, as if raising the gender issue would be perceived as harming or detracting from the Palestinian cause or weaken the Palestinian empowerment process. Facilitators in the classroom often feel that it is neither the right time nor the place to open up discussions on gender stereotypes. For example, Jewish facilitators might not want the Palestinians to feel attacked by a discussion of gender issues, feeling that it is a sensitive topic that will allow Jews to be seen as significantly more progressive than Palestinians.

When the complexity of gender and national identities arises in discussions, the facilitators tend to differentiate between sexist and racist stereotypes. Subsequently they tend to place more importance on the racist stereotypes, ignoring those based on gender. This, even if well explained and reasoned, has the effect of legitimizing, affirming, enhancing, and aggravating gender-based stereotypes. Such stereotypes push the young women who participate in dialogue processes into social roles of either serving and caring "mothers" who protect "their men," or of sexy lovers for men's gratification. They are denied being perceived as subjects with needs, interests, and wants. Thus, such attitudes clearly hinder the intended process of stereotype-breaking. Accommodating sexist/racist behavior and language and the refusal to address gender stereotypes reinforces abusive attitudes rather than questioning and opposing them. Knowledgeable facilitators might introduce skills and language so as to help participants deal with gender matters, recognizing the impact of this unresolved sub-conflict on the prospects for conflict resolution.

Follow-up research on gender stereotypes

Based on the assumption that innovative dialogue processes can integrate gender as a major component by raising it as a topic, putting it on the official agenda, and by allocating time and other group resources to its discussion, I conducted further research in an international setting at international training centers, commercial companies that engaged in a gender training, and at UPEACE, asking MA students of peace studies, gender, media, and peace education and human rights to draw a man and a woman in gender-isolated groups of five to seven participants (altogether there were 24 smaller working groups on whose results the findings here are based). I used content analysis based on participatory self-ethnography and on observation and interviews with ten of the participants.

In the workshops participants were asked to draw a man and a woman in 15 minutes. The time pressure is an important part of the method presented here, in order to prevent students from trying to second-guess what might be politically correct. For this reason, I often used blocks of ice cream, as mentioned above, and asked students to sculpt a man and a woman. This forced the participants to work fast for 10–15 minutes and to prevent too much reflection on social expectations. Each group would receive ice cream, colored whipped cream, and candy decorations and was asked to start sculpting. The joint artistic endeavor, in addition to the excitement over the unconventional work in combination with the limited time they had before the ice-cream melted, brought to the surface the deepest stereotypes of the self and the Other.

Women's groups, when asked to draw different genders, would first draw a woman—representing themselves—and then a man, while most male groups chose to draw a woman first and then a man. The depictions of the woman were either the "holy mother" taking care of a baby, or a woman as sexual object. Branded goods and shopping were themes that came up in every group in this context, most pronouncedly when it came to the depictions of women by women.

Almost none of the characters drawn by the students were talking. When speech acts were depicted, men were assertive, giving orders, while women were nagging or chatting about nothing of consequence; speech thus had positive connotations when associated with men and negative connotations in respect to women.

The male image was drawn by men and often also by women as hypermasculine without a shirt on or alternatively in a suit. Sometimes there was a combination between hypermasculinity signified by muscles and the professional power uniform of the suit, hinting at a white-collar job; frequently men were also shown working out and drinking. Participants stated that alcoholic drinks did not reflect a stereotype since men often drink more than women. This logic shows the difficulty in initiating a transformative dialogue about gender stereotypes.

These traditional gender-based stereotypes are widely shared among students who tend to hold negative stereotypes of women in management and leadership positions (Duehr and Bono, 2006). For example, the stereotype that was often drawn of women is one who is "wasteful" with her husband's money, spending it on clothes and branded goods, while men are seen by social cultural norms as those creating and saving the family's wealth (Hentschel, Heilman, & Peus 2019). Common sayings such as "she is an expensive girlfriend/wife" are often heard within international organizations in regard to women, as reported by Mary, an international aid worker. Sara, one of the gender workshop participants, explained her group's drawings, saying "we are all working in the same job but in order to know that we are loved we would like him [pointing at their drawing of the man] to spend money on us." Everybody in the class laughed at this statement; no one reflected aloud on the fact that it reinforced a gender stereotype.

How can teachers encourage a reflective process and enable a dialogue about gender-based stereotypes in order to reduce these and perhaps change students' perspectives? If we compare the drawings of a man and a woman to the drawings that were produced for a project developing a children's book on human rights,[6] we can recognize convergences. To begin with, refugees or those whose human rights are in jeopardy are depicted as small and often exposed (for instance as a snail whose shell had been crushed). What does it imply when we consider that men and women in the workshops were often drawn as exposed? What did the participants think about themselves? When asked, participants answered that bodily differences were at the core of gender presentations, that they wanted to draw what "others might think." In addition, they used a biological discourse, claiming that men are strong and powerful while women are seductive, sexy and motherly "in their core being."

The drawings and sculptures were even more interesting and complex when groups were aware and had knowledge of gender-based stereotypes, the gendered division of labor, and beauty complexes, seeking to present men and women as equal. In the professional setting of a training day in a commercial company in Israel, eight men and nine women sculpted figures in ice cream. The women's group created a man and a woman who looked roughly the same apart from a pink ribbon on the woman's neck. A conversation ensued as to how women would like to be represented and questions were raised about femininity and whether a female figure that is identical to the male encompasses womanhood and femininity and, moreover, what constitutes femininity in the workplace. Women shared stories about how important it is for them to look nice and to be considered beautiful (rather than or additional to smart). They also confronted the men's group that sculpted a naked woman with very large breasts, pointing out that this suggested they were judged based on their looks. The men represented themselves with an image of a naked torso wearing a tie.

In light of these findings it is important to note that the students who participated in the workshops described were all professionals in leadership positions, peace and development workers, or studying for master's degrees at UPEACE. It is therefore likely that they will all have been exposed to a multitude of strong, powerful women, and are aware of different female lifestyles. Why, then, did they choose to represent men as powerful and in control and women mostly as mothers and sexy shoppers who talk too much? When asked, the participants and students said that they wanted to represent what they call "typical women," meaning a generic representation of femininity, rather than themselves; that when they think of women, they think of local women who are different from themselves. A few came to me after the debriefing to thank me for what was left unsaid in the workshop. They reported that they are under heavy pressure to succeed in their studies by their families, who had invested a lot of money to send them to university, and yet also at the same time to find an eligible husband and get married. They felt that the stereotypical gender representation of women (themselves) was reflective of this tension. When asked why they had not shared this during the workshop they answered that they had been embarrassed to admit pressure to find a husband for fear of appearing desperate and having others look down on them as a result.

Conclusion

Halabi and Zak, in their book *When the Present Are Absent*, further develop conflict theory and related approaches. They highlight the fact that observing one's own stereotypes can lead to distress and extreme discomfort (Halabi and Zak, 2006). However, according to colonialist theories the only way to bring about change in views and behavior is to encourage frustration, mainly within the hegemonic group (Memmi, 1991). This kind of discomfort and frustration that often leads to resistance and even antagonism could be witnessed within the gender dialogue groups during the drawing exercise. It was difficult to talk about the stereotypes that acquired a life of their own when put to paper: "It is horrible, we are so sexist toward women and men!" said Tima, a student at UPEACE during the drawing session. The images enabled the participants to look the stereotypes "in the eye" and begin talking, reflecting upon them, and to think of separate and joint strategies of how to deal with them.

While Halabi and Zak (2006) argue that breaking up stereotypes is a difficult and slow undertaking and that basic assumptions often remain static, social psychologist Patricia Devine is convinced that it is fairly easy to break stereotypes in what she terms a "truthful dialog encounter": an encounter that looks at people as human beings rather than enemies (Devine, Ashby, & Buswell, 2000). The method described here, while fully appreciating the findings of Halabi and Zak, tried to use Devine's approach to effect change. That it was successful was borne out by all the facilitators, students, and participants who were interviewed after the classes or workshops, stating that they changed their view on the Other group(s).

Some participants talked at length about their self-stereotypes and concluded that these are the hardest to break. When analyzing stereotypes, they would rarely begin with the stereotypes they held about themselves and their own groups, either because these were too close to home or simply because they were not aware of the fact that they harbored such stereotypes. In turn, the invisibility of such self-stereotypes makes it more difficult to deconstruct stereotypes about the Other.

The practice of drawing stereotypes of the self and the Other and comparing and contrasting them within and across groups enabled a truthful and deep dialogue on questions of identity, ethnicity, and nationality, intersecting with gender. The practice might be of use facilitating a dialogue around immigration, discrimination, and the exclusion of different people from diverse groups such as people with disabilities, members of the LGBTQIA+ community, and religious and ethnic minorities.

Notes

1 The participants in the groups were asked to divide according to gender—any gender—they chose. Most groups divided into men and women, while some tried to form a gender queer group but, in all cases, later in the division process affiliated themselves with either the women or the men group.
2 In brief, when people hear an expression and automatically assign a gender to the concept, e.g., associating "doctor" with a man, "nurse" with a woman, "love and care" with motherhood.
3 Muna (all names were changed) (34), female Palestinian facilitator interviewed on August 14, 2007.
4 Ibid.
5 The attempt to reduce scope or measurements of the female body by squeezing it into shapewear.
6 See Chapter 3.

References

Adichie, C. 2009. Transcript of "The Danger of a Single Story". [online] Ted.com. Available at: https://www.ted.com/talks/chimamanda_adichie_the_danger_of_a_single_story/transcript?language=en [Accessed March 22, 2019].

Banaji, M.R. & Hardin, C.D. 1996. "Automatic Stereotyping." *Psychological Science* 7(3): 136–141. https://doi.org/10.1111/j.1467-9280.1996.tb00346.x

Butler, J. 1993. *Bodies that Matter: On the Discursive Limits of "Sex"*. New York: Routledge.

Brown-Jeffy, S., & Cooper, J. 2011. "Toward a Conceptual Framework of Culturally Relevant Pedagogy: An Overview of the Conceptual and Theoretical Literature." *Teacher Education Quarterly* 38(1): 65–84. Retrieved from http://www.jstor.org/stable/23479642

Campbell, A., Shirley, L., & Caygill, L. 2002. "Sex-typed Preferences in Three Domains: Do Two-year-olds Need Cognitive Variables?" *British Journal of Psychology* 93(2): 203–217.

Chiu, C., Hong, Y., Lam, I.C., Fu, J. H.-Y., Tong, J.Y., & Lee, V.S. 1998. "Stereotyping and Self-Presentation: Effects of Gender Stereotype Activation." *Group Processes & Intergroup Relations* 1(1): 81–96. https://doi.org/10.1177/1368430298011007

de Beauvoir, Simone. 1949. *The Second Sex*. New York: Vintage Books.

Duehr, E.E. and Bono, J.E. 2006. "Men, Women, and Managers: Are Stereotypes Finally Changing?" *Personal Psychology* 59: 815–846.

Devine, P.G., AshbyP., & Buswell, B.N. 2000. *Breaking the Prejudice Habit: Progress and Obstacles. Reducing Prejudice and Discrimination*. Mahwah, NJ: Lawrence Erlbaum Associates.

Enns, C.Z., & Forrest, L.M. 2005. "Toward Defining and Integrating Multicultural and Feminist Pedagogies." In C.Z. Enns & A.L. Sinacore (eds.), *Teaching and Social Justice: Integrating Multicultural and Feminist Theories in the Classroom*, 3–23. Washington, DC: American Psychological Association.

Frederickson, B.L. & Roberts, T. 1997. "Objectification Theory: Toward Understanding Women's Lived Experiences and Mental Health Risks." *Psychology of Women Quarterly* 21: 173–206.

Friedman, A. 2013. *Blind to Sameness: Sex, Perception and the Social Construction of Male and Female Bodies*. Chicago: University of Chicago Press.

Goffman, E. 1956. *The Presentation of Self in Everyday Life*. Edinburgh: University of Edinburgh, Social Sciences Research Centre.

Greenleaf, C. 2005*Sex Roles* 52: 51. https://doi.org/10.1007/s11199-005-1193-8

Grogan, S. 1999. *Body Image: Understanding Body Dissatisfaction in Men, Women, and Children*. London: Routledge.

Gunderson, M. 1989. "Male–Female Wage Differentials and Policy Responses." *Journal of Economic Literature* 27(1), 46–72.

Halabi, R., and Zak, M. 2006. *When the Present Are Absent: Jewish–Palestinian Youth Encounters in the School for Peace*. Jerusalem: School for Peace Research Center. (In Hebrew.)

Hentschel, T., Heilman, M.E., & Peus, C.V. 2019. *The Multiple Dimensions of Gender Stereotypes: A Current Look at Men's and Women's Characterizations of Others and Themselves*. Northwestern University, United States: Front Psychology.
hooks, b. 1990. *Yearning: Race, Gender & Cultural Politics*. Boston: South End Press.
Jones, J.M. 1997. *Prejudice and Racism*. New York: McGraw-Hill.
Levinas, E. 1974. *Autrement qu'être ou au-delà de l'essence*. (Otherwise than Being or Beyond Essence.) Translated 1998. Pittsburgh, PA: Duquesne University Press.
Major, B., Quinton, W.J., & Schmader, T. 2003. "Attributions to Discrimination and Self-esteem: Impact of Group Identification and Situational Ambiguity." *Journal of Experimental Social Psychology* 39(3): 220–231.
Memmi, A. 1991. *The Colonizer and the Colonized*, Boston:Beacon Press.
Neander, K. & Scott, C. 2006. "Important Meetings with Important Persons: Narratives from Families Facing Adversity and Their Key Figures." *Qualitative Social Work: Research and Practice* 5: 295–311.
Reinharz, S. & Davidman, L. 1992. *Feminist Methods in Social Research*. New York: Oxford University Press.
RubleD.N., Martin, C.L. & Berenbaum, S. 1998. "Gender Development." In D. Kuhn & R. Siegler (eds.) *Handbook of Child Sex Roles Psychology: Cognition, Perception and Language*. 6th ed. New York: Wiley.
Solórzano, D.G., & Yosso, T.J. 2002. "Critical Race Methodology: Counter-Storytelling as an Analytical Framework for Education Research." *Qualitative Inquiry* 8(1): 23–44. https://doi.org/10.1177/107780040200800103
Sonnenschein, N., Halabi, R., & Friedman, A. 1998. "Israeli–Palestinian Workshops: Legitimation of National Identity and Change in Power Relationships." In E. Weiner (ed.) *The Handbook of Interethnic Coexistence*, 600–615. New York: Continuum.
Stiehm, J. 1994. "The Protected, the Protector, the Defender." In J. Boulder (ed.) *Living with Contradictions: Controversies in Feminist Social Ethics*, 582–592. Boulder, CO: Westview Press.
Williams, J.E., Bennett, S.M., & Best, D.L. 1975. "Awareness and Expression of Sex Stereotypes in Young Children." *Developmental Psychology* 11: 635–642.

Index

accent 3, 9
ableism 19
academic 4, 5, 26, 55; career 56; jargon 6, 24, 29–32, 46; publishing 5; writing, traditional conventions of 5, 31
adultism 19
Adwan, Sami 11
Africa 10, 39, 59
African American
ageism 19
apartheid 10
Arab 18
Arabic 10, 12–18, 54–63, 65, 74
Asia 18, 33–4, 39, 54, 59
assimilation 17, 27, 47
attitudes 28–9, 38, 56, 81

Bar-On, Dan 11
beauty 7, 15, 83; standards 29, 33, 34, 73; myth 24, 30, 33, 69; ideal 29
Bechdel test 51, 66
bento boxes 43, 44
Beauvoir, Simone de 15, 34
Bible, the 9
biological 34, 35, 37, 39, 83
binary 73; cultural 5; gender 23, 28, 68; racial; thought patterns 4
black 33, 61; children 10, 51; perception 17; women 3
body, the 24, 29, 33–7, 41–5, 78
Bosnia-Herzegovina 8

capital: financial 25; cultural 25, 30, 55–6

Cambodia 39, 54
children's literature 11, 19, 50–2, 57–61, 65, 70, 83
chocolate 39
Christianity 54, 10, 60, 64, 74
class 2, 9, 24–7, 30–2, 36, 56, 79
classism 19, 69
colonialism/colonialist 55, 72, 77, 81–84
collaborative writing 50, 57
color 3, 33, 35, 71
communication technology 4
conflict 27, 39, 52–5, 73, 84; Israel-Palestine 9; and names 10–14; regions of 5, 11, 13; classroom 6, 19
Congo, Democratic Republic of the 8, 36
conservative/conservatism 8, 72, 14
contraception 39
cosmetics 33
Crenshaw, Kimberlé 3, 5, 6, 26; *see also* "double oppression"
creativity 18
culture 4–7, 17–19, 27–9, 60–3, 74; hegemonic 18, 29; and language 57; and tension 6
curriculum 5, 19, 29, 47, 52, 64, 76

daily life 7, 19
"dead metaphors" (Lakoff & Johnson) 7
development 9, 19, 33, 46, 47, 50, 51, 65, 69, 70, 71, 73; international 10, 13, 17, 23, 24, 41, 84; interventions 3, 19
dialogue 17–19, 27, 30–1, 54, 63, 69, 79, 82; classroom 18, 25, 29, 31–5, 41,

Index

52; in conflict 53, 75–6, 84; creating space for 29, 52–4, 73, 77, 81–5
diaspora 13
discourse 18, 32–4, 41, 60, 79; analysis 23, 29, 37, 50–1; and power 12, 29, 31–3, 44, 55, 69, 71; hegemonic 14, 29, 57–8, 74–5; shifts in 19–20, 29, 42, 46, 65, 81
discrimination 3, 4, 16–8, 30, 37–9, 62, 85
"double oppression" (Crenshaw) 3
driving; and women in Saudi Arabia 61
Druze 74

economics 8–9, 26, 31, 36–8, 40–2, 52–3, 78
education 2–6, 30, 53, 57, 62, 70; critical 9, 25, 31, 40, 51; and gender 31, 43, 47, 53; intersectional 3, 18, 32, 50, 58, 64; peace 10, 19, 23–4, 52–6, 63–8, 82
emotions 3, 5, 9, 11
English 55–8, 63; as a hegemonic language 7, 10, 24, 31; native speakers of 8, 31
environment 8, 36, 52–4, 70–3
ethics 33
Ethiopia 58
ethnic 12, 18, 25–8, 57–9, 85; tension 6, 7, 77, 80; cleansing 10; conflict 8, 9, 13, 74; discrimination 17, 27, 52; visibility 31, 33, 51, 71, 76; ethnocentric 12, 72
ethnography 6
Europe 17, 18, 33
exploitation 26, 34, 40

Facebook 4
feminine 28, 29, 33, 34, 35; behaviour 30, 32, 34, 35, 36, 75; names 14; products 33, 37, 38, 41, 42, 44, 70; *see also* pink tax
feminist 24, 26, 29; critical pedagogy 5, 23–9, 32, 40, 50–1, 69; criticism 34; perception of 30, 42; practice 30, 41; research 5, 72, 74; theory 27, 29, 34, 46
France 16–8

Gaza 10, 59
geography 9, 12–14, 32
gender: and names 14–15; compulsory courses in 16–18, 23–4; equity 20, 53; everyday object analysis 19–20, 23, 27–8; identity 7, 23, 27, 77; (in)equality 29–30; pedagogy 5, 10, 24, 25; practical 23, 26, 34; perspectives 24; resistance to 23, 29–30; roles 34
Germany 9, 17, 62
government 29
globalization 33, 10, 28, 34, 58

habits 13
Haifa 10
Hebrew 9, 13, 14, 17, 55, 56, 57, 58, 60, 61, 63, 64
herstory 52
heritage 17, 10, 19; Jewish-Israeli 9; Palestinian 9
heteronormativity 45, 64, 73
hegemony 11, 14, 28, 29, 31, 32, 33, 44, 57, 59
hierarchy 32, 26, 38, 40, 52, 60, 61, 68
hijab 61
historical 2, 5, 7, 9, 11, 13, 14, 25, 28, 31, 32, 35, 75, 81; education; narrative
homeland 9, 13; connection with; historical 9; Israeli 14; Palestinian 13
human rights 20, 54, 55; education (HRE) 50, 51–8, 64–8, 73, 82–3; Universal Declaration of 59; violations of 59–62, 83

identity 85; and names 18; gender 27, 30, 69, 70, 75–78, 85; cultural 7, 17, 27, 36, 63; ethnic 17, 71, 75–6, 80, 85; group 17, 31, 50, 77; intersectional 2–8, 17, 25, 29; individual 27–9, 57, 69, 78; national 9, 75–7, 80–5; religious 17; sexual 85
ideology 4–5, 8–9, 20, 29, 40, 72
Instagram 4
integration 17, 18, 28, 58
intersectionality 3–5, 8, 19–26, 29, 30; in education 20, 40, 51, 71, 74; awareness of 32, 45, 72, 80

Iraq 8, 18
Ireland, Republic of 8
Islam 18
Israel 8–12, 14, 23, 62, 65, 69, 74–6; Arab schools in 54, 74; hegemonic language in 56, 58, 61; Social Change and Art College, Netanya 16, 51, 54; sociopolitical tensions in 57, 60, 79

Japan 33, 43, 54, 61; women in 42, 43, 44
Jerusalem 62
jihad 12
job market 17
Jordan 17

kindness (Clegg & Rowland) 4
knowledge 14, 24, 31, 40–3; hidden 8, 9, 53, 56; transmission of 4, 25, 27, 32, 52; production of 2, 19, 20, 28–31, 51, 69, 74

language: academic, resistance to, 32, 47; accessibility of 32, 33, 46, 56, 61, 62; and conflict 11, 17, 81; and culture 7, 17, 60, 66, 68, 74; and power 11, 17, 31, 42, 50, 55, 60, 65, 69, 71; hegemonic 24, 31, 39, 46, 52, 55–8, 61–5
Latin America 18, 58
legitimacy 9, 60, 46, 58
Latino 18
learning: experiential 20, 28, 37, 40–6, 52, 68; goals 27, 24–6, 31–2, 55; material 5, 29, 55; rote 19; refusal of 12, 30, 31; styles 5, 25, 33, 54; traditional 5
LGBTQIA+ 45, 64, 85, 87
liberalism 5, 8, 14, 80

male fragility 41
marginalized: groups 4, 9, 10–12, 56–7, 75, 78
masculine 78; behavior 28, 34–6; gaze 39; identity 10–16, 29, 33, 78, 82; status symbols 38, 40
mediation; process of 4, 5, 13
#metoo 41–42

"meta-metaphors" (Lakoff & Johnson) 8, 13
migrants: first generation 17; second generation 17, 18, 63
migration 17, 18, 55, 58, 63, 85
marriage 30, 64; arranged; mixed 10; proposals 40
media 29, 82, 37, 41, 52, 66, 68
memory cultures 13
militant 12
monogamy 40
motherhood 44
multiculturalism 24, 29

names: advantages 2; analysis 6, 12, 14, 15, 18; conflict- sensitive 6, 10, 13, 14, 17, 44, 60; gender-sensitive 7, 15; feminine 7, 13, 14, 15, 16; implications of 1, 6, 10, 15, 16, 17; masculine 14, 15, 16; meaning app 6, 10, 13, 14, 15; pronunciation 7, 10, 1, 15, 18; spelling of 7, 9, 15, 61
name-story sharing 2, 6, 7, 9, 11, 16, 18, 19; practices of 6; narratives 13, 19, 25, 27
Netherlands, the 61
norms 26, 34, 43, 52, 83
Northern Ireland 8

objectification 37–9, 69, 78
open source materials 57, 61
oppression 26, 30–9, 44, 46, 52, 75
other; humanization of 7, 11; self and 12, 19, 69, 70–4, 85
othering: mechanisms of 19

parenthood 26
Palestine 9, 11, 13
Palestinian Israeli 12, 13
pedagogy 23–7; 32–8; critical 1, 5, 52, 53; culturally relevant 5; peace 10; perception 5
peace: accords 14; education 13–4, 19, 50–3, 70, 68
pink tax 35
pornography 44
power 35–8, 53, 65–9; dynamics 5, 12, 14, 18, 72; relations 25, 26, 28, 30, 31–7, 40–44, 51, 78, 75; and language 55–61

pregnancy 34
prejudice 6, 19, 80, 69, 70, 71, 80
privilege 11, 18, 36, 45, 70, 72, 78
promiscuity 79, 80
politics 29, 32, 43, 50, 71
public sphere 29, 39, 44, 54

queer 45, 64

racism 17
racial theory 19
rape culture 41, 44, 45; victim-blaming 42; politics of silence 43
refugee 83, 3, 6, 11, 17, 19, 61, 62, 72, 78, 83
religion 7–12, 17–19, 26–30, 64–5, 78, 85; and conflict 8
rituals 39, 29, 40
risk 39, 73, 18

Saudi Arabia 61
safe space 24, 27, 73, 46
sexism 16, 69, 80
sexual: harassment 41–45, 69; identity 26; orientation 19, 25, 26, 64; symbols 38
sexuality 28–9, 44
sisterhood 41
smoking; and culture 37; and gender 36, 79
social media 4, 41
social: constructs 19, 25, 68, 70–2; justice 20, 26; mechanisms 25; mobility 58

socialization 7, 35
South Africa 10, 15
status 23, 36–9, 43, 58, 60, 72
stereotypes 2, 32, 70–9, 80–5
storytelling 19, 28
students 3,5, 19, 31
Sudan 10
Switzerland 38, 61
Syria 9, 13
symbolism 9, 12–15, 27–8, 30–9, 42–4

teachers 19, 40–2, 51–4, 62–6
terrorism 6, 12
trauma 43–5, 51, 56
truth 28–9, 51, 69, 85
Twitter 4

USA 11, 14, 16, 18
UN Security Council 24

Valentine's Day 39
values 7–8, 15, 17, 28–9, 52, 54, 75

war 12, 14
wealth 8, 57, 83
West Bank 59
white 10, 18, 30, 33, 80; feminism 30
women's studies 29, 46
#whydidntireport 41

YouTube 4, 40

Zionism 9

For Product Safety Concerns and Information please contact our EU representative GPSR@taylorandfrancis.com
Taylor & Francis Verlag GmbH, Kaufingerstraße 24, 80331 München, Germany

www.ingramcontent.com/pod-product-compliance
Lightning Source LLC
Chambersburg PA
CBHW051758230426
43670CB00012B/2344